Comedy: A Very Short Introduction

VERY SHORT INTRODUCTIONS are for anyone wanting a stimulating and accessible way in to a new subject. They are written by experts, and have been published in more than 25 languages worldwide.

The series began in 1995, and now represents a wide variety of topics in history, philosophy, religion, science, and the humanities. The VSI library now contains more than 300 volumes—a Very Short Introduction to everything from ancient Egypt and Indian philosophy to conceptual art and cosmology—and will continue to grow in a variety of disciplines.

## VERY SHORT INTRODUCTIONS AVAILABLE NOW:

Available soon:

For more information visit our website
www.oup.com/vsi/

Matthew Bevis

# COMEDY

## A Very Short Introduction

OXFORD
UNIVERSITY PRESS

# OXFORD
UNIVERSITY PRESS

Great Clarendon Street, Oxford, OX2 6DP,
United Kingdom

Oxford University Press is a department of the University of Oxford.
It furthers the University's objective of excellence in research, scholarship,
and education by publishing worldwide. Oxford is a registered trade mark of
Oxford University Press in the UK and in certain other countries

© Matthew Bevis 2013

The moral rights of the author have been asserted

First Edition published in 2013

Impression: 2

British Library Cataloguing in Publication Data

Data available

Library of Congress Cataloging in Publication Data

Data available

ISBN 978-0-19-960171-4

Printed in Great Britain by
Ashford Colour Press Ltd, Gosport, Hampshire

Ils abordèrent la Comédie—qui est l'école
des nuances.
Flaubert, *Bouvard and Pecuchet* (1881)

# Contents

# Acknowledgements

I am grateful to the Leverhulme Trust for awarding me a Philip Leverhulme Prize from 2008 to 2010; this book emerged from the reading and thinking I began during that time. For conversations and questions I would like to thank Derek Attridge, Kathryn Bevis, Judith Buchanan, Jonathan Butler, Matthew Campbell, Kenneth Clarke, Ziad Elmarsafy, Jean Holloway, Alex Houen, Freya Johnston, Hermione Lee, Angela Leighton, Andrew Miller, Julia Knowles, Nicholas Knowles, Marcus Nevitt, Erica Sheen, and Marcus Waithe. I am indebted to Luciana O'Flaherty at the Press, who supported the book at the outset, and to Emma Marchant, Andrea Keegan, and Kerstin Demata, who saw it through the final stages. Many thanks, too, to the anonymous OUP readers for their helpful comments on the book as it took shape.

I am especially grateful to Hugh Haughton, Adam Phillips, Seamus Perry, John Mullan, and Rebecca Knowles for inspiration and encouragement; they each read earlier drafts and offered many valuable suggestions and ideas. Any unwitting comedy arising from the remaining errors is my fault.

This book is dedicated to Rebecca, who laughed and humoured me along the way.

# List of illustrations

Comedy

# Curtain raiser

When you were six you thought mistress meant to put your shoes on the wrong feet. Now you are older and know it can mean many things, but essentially it means to put your shoes on the wrong feet.

Lorrie Moore, 'How to Be an Other Woman' (1985)

What does comedy mean? The *Oxford English Dictionary* defines it as 'a stage-play of light and amusing character', before conceding that the term extends to other kinds of 'humorous invention' as well as being used figuratively with regard to 'action or incidents in real life'. The same widening of horizons occurs in the *Dictionary*'s definition of 'the comic': 'the comic side of drama, of life, etc.'. The movement from 'drama' to 'life' to 'etc.' covers quite a bit of terrain, and the dictionary writers' need for latitude has been shared by others. In Plato's *Philebus*, Socrates speaks of comedy 'not only on the stage, but on the greater stage of human life; and so in endless other cases'. Endless? Hardly a cheering prospect for those in search of a clear-cut definition. It almost sounds as though thinking about comedy or humour *as* categories may be some kind of category error. The cartoonist Saul Steinberg hinted as much: 'trying to define humour is one of the definitions of humour'. Better, then, to come right out with it and say that comedy can mean many things, but essentially it means to put your shoes on the wrong feet.

Taxonomic tangles aside, comedy's varied incarnations raise diverse but related sets of questions. One line of enquiry might focus on comedy as a theatrical and literary genre, and ask: What are the form's main features? How has it retained consistency and changed over time? But taking into account the *OED*'s sense of comedy as a broader impulse at work and play in life, we could also ask: How can humour be used? When do we laugh, and why? What is it that speakers as well as writers enjoy—and risk—when they tell a joke, indulge in bathos, talk nonsense, or encourage irony? This book pursues both types of question. By the 19th century, after all, one proprietor of a Punch booth could note ruefully that 'Everyone's funny now-a-days, and they like the comic business.' Funny business plies its trade across the boundaries between recognized, institutionalized forms of writing and more experimental, popular kinds of entertainment, so it's helpful to think about comedy as a literary genre and as a range of non-literary phenomena, experiences, and events. This means focusing not only on the classics of comic drama, prose fiction, and poetry, but also on forms of pantomime, circus, comic opera, silent cinema, music hall, stand-up acts, rom-coms, and sketch shows. In addition, there are countless moments when comedy-as-performance breaks out off-stage—people tell witty anecdotes, play on words, do funny walks and impressions, and so on.

Given the topic's range, this book will need to be a very fast as well as a very short introduction. Some orientation may be useful before the curtain goes up. Many guides to comedy try to get readers from A to B by offering a potted history of the dramatic form (from Aristophanes to Beckett), or by providing a run-through of theoretical perspectives (from Aristotle to Bakhtin). This introduction is not a history of comedy, although individual chapters are structured in a broadly chronological way to draw out a sense of how the mode has developed from the Greeks to the present. I occasionally succumb to the temptation to write things like 'comedy relies on X' or 'the comic revels in Y'. This is not to say that comedy is held up as some kind of Eternal Principle rather than as a historical phenomenon (what comedy has meant to different periods and cultures has varied). But whilst comedy takes shape in time, discernable ideas and patterns recur over time. I'm interested here in thinking about what might be termed the repertoires of comedy—with comedy conceived as an instinct that can exceed specified boundaries, as a container for expectations and surprises, and as a way of encountering the world.

The book is organized around a series of interrelated topics: beginnings, bodies, characters, plots, power, pain, and endings. My aim is to allow comic theory and practice to talk to one another, and to encourage comparisons between different periods and modes from high and low culture. The devil is in the comic detail, so I'll be leading by examples, quoting quickly and often, trying whenever possible to let comedy tell its own story. Not that the examples are unrelated to precepts: certain people, scenes, moments, and styles are chosen and examined as representatives of larger debates. The case studies are meant to support (and test) the broader theories and generalizations.

A *very* short introduction should suit this subject. Brevity is the soul of wit. Buster Keaton told his father that a good comedy could be written on a penny postcard. Nothing worse than labouring a joke by explaining it, after all, because a joke—as the philosopher Theodor Lipps pointed out—always 'says what it says...in too few words'. From the ridicule of Socrates in Aristophanes's *Clouds* to the ribbing of the Crane brothers in *Frasier*, the comic imagination has frequently picked on intellectuals, hair-splitters, pedants, and other animals drawn to prolixity. Max Eastman rightly observed that 'the correct explanation of a joke not only does not sound funny, but it does not sound like a correct explanation'. Still, if comedy deals in failures of intelligence then it should exercise ours; we can take comedy seriously without taking it solemnly. Ludwig Wittgenstein claimed that 'a serious and good philosophical work could be written that would consist entirely of *jokes*'. This is perhaps because jokes are one way of inviting us to think about what we know—and what we think we know. The surprise that accompanies getting a joke can prompt us to wonder about the expectations that were toyed with to get us there, and what these expectations may tell us about ourselves. Paolo Virno has recently argued that 'Every joke puts into focus...the variety of alternatives that come forth in applying a norm.' This in turn can encourage reflection on whether we want to inhabit or resist that norm.

It may be that rumours of comedy's subversive, radical nature have been greatly exaggerated. Indeed, certain strands of Marxist thought see it as yet another opiate for the masses; Adorno and Horkheimer bemoan the Culture Industry's use of jokes and comedy as a narcotic, lamenting how 'it makes laughter the instrument of the fraud practised on happiness'. Some laughs can be like this, but not all. Besides, comedy is about more than jokes, and it needn't always arouse laughter. Several forms of thought and expression that are not necessarily jokey or laugh-out-loud funny—vocabularies of 'folly', for instance, or 'fertility', or 'the absurd'—seem to move within the orbit of comedy, and I'll reflect on these relations and others along the way. For now, though, one opening hypothesis is that study of the comic involves a consideration of 'that which is laughable' (with the provisos that the 'laughable' may or may not lead to laughter, and that, if it does, this laughter can be hard to gauge).

In Anita Loos's *Gentlemen Prefer Blondes* (1925), when Lorelei Lee enjoys Piggie's jokes—'So then Piggie laughed very, very loud. So of course I laughed very, very loud and I told Piggie he was wonderful the way he could tell jokes'—it is delightfully uncertain whom, exactly, the joke is on. Is Lorelei laughing at Piggie, or are we laughing at her, or—last but not least—is the book laughing at us, coyly counselling against too knowing an attitude to the heroine? Sigmund Freud (or, rather, 'Dr Froyd', a man Lorelei will herself meet during her travels) suggests that 'we scarcely ever know what it is we are laughing at in a joke, even though we can settle it afterwards by analytic investigation'. More recently, the philosopher Ronald de Sousa has argued that, when it comes to laughter, analysis stops nowhere: 'If we can answer the question "What did you *intend* by laughing?" then it was not genuine laughter.' So perhaps an introduction to comedy should savour the pleasure of its subject by keeping questions open, even as it tries to tease out what the salient questions might be. When Federico Fellini was asked to comment on what his documentary-fantasy *Clowns* (1970) was getting at, he replied: 'When I ask a good question, I don't care about the answer.'

# Chapter 1
## In the beginning...

'Wait. Let me think a minute,' you said.

...then you made a brilliant pun.

We gave a thunderclap of laughter.

Flustered, your helpers vanished one by one;

And through the conversational spaces, after,

we caught—back, back, far, far,—

the glinting birthday of a fractious star.

Elizabeth Bishop, 'The Wit' (1956)

## A star is born

Comedy can offer us reassurance about where we stand. A shared joke is a shared world. Yet comic instincts also invite us to think up new worlds, and have often spoken most eloquently to those who are keen to try things out. Glossing her poem, Bishop explained that 'making a pun is unlike logical thought; it fractures, in a contrary way—as we might imagine the birth of a star, or creation itself'. Calling the pun itself 'brilliant' (from *brillare*, 'to shine') is the poet's way of assisting at the act of creation; she practises as well as describes lightning and enlightening wit. This creation story—let there be laughter—is a variation on ancient cosmologies that sing of gods creating the world by laughing. The Bible, too, makes an association between laughter and astonishing, miraculous births, as the first laugh in Genesis comes from Abraham: he 'fell upon his face, and laughed, and said in his heart, Shall a child be born unto him that is an hundred years old? and shall Sarah, that is ninety years old, bear?' (17:17) Indeed she shall. She will bear Isaac, whose own name is a punning echo of his parents' initial reactions (*Yichaq* means 'he will laugh' in Hebrew). 'And Sarah said, God hath made me to laugh, so that all that hear will laugh with me' (21:6).

'In the beginning was the pun,' intones Samuel Beckett's Murphy. Comic imaginations have often circled around the idea of origins, but—like a pun, which teases doubleness from singularity—the beginning of comedy itself is tricky to pin down to a specific location. The etymological roots of the word hint at the obscure origins of the form. Some have argued for comedy's home in *kome* ('country village'), but the more likely derivation is from *komos*, a complex word best translated by Kenneth Dover: 'a noisy, happy, drunken procession'. Then add the suffix *ody* ('song'), and a picture emerges of a boozed-up bunch making a song and dance about things (see Figure 1).

1. *Komos*

The *Tractatus Coislinianus* manuscript provides a neat Aristotelian definition of comedy—'the imitation of an action which is funny'—and notes that 'its mother is laughter'. But who's the father? Aristotle speculated in his *Poetics* that Attic comedy came down from the abusive iambic poetry of those who led forth phallic processions. When coupled with the drinking, this lineage takes us to the door of Dionysus, the Greek god of wine, pleasure, and festivity. It has been claimed—most famously by the classical scholar Francis Cornford—that comedy descends from Dionysian and phallic rituals in and around Athens, and that the plays of Aristophanes (the earliest extant examples of Western comic drama) model themselves on seasonal vegetation and fertility rites. From this perspective, comic riot is predicated on ritual. Its distinguishing features include: scurrilous mockery as a form of life-affirming purification; rebirths from death, along with the resurrection of the new year from the old; and licensed displays of indecency as the sign of procreative energies.

Although these claims about the aetiology of comedy have been subject to much dispute, Attic drama certainly breathes freely in this atmosphere. Performers wore large, artificial penises and grotesque masks (there was a long tradition of associating masked impersonation with worship of Dionysus). The institutional birthdate of comedy is 486 BC, when space was made for it in the dramatic competitions at the festivals in Athens in honour of Dionysus. The very performance of these plays was part of a religious observance; during the City Dionysia a statue of the patron god, along with the priest of Dionysus himself, oversaw the dramatic action. Yet while Aristophanic comedy flirts with authorized customs, it also delights in sending them up by including parodies of religious rites from within the play itself. In *Frogs* (405 BC), one character breaks from the action to appeal to the boss in the front row: 'Oh, Mister Priest, protect me! Remember that drink we're going to have after the show!' The line is uttered by none other than Dionysus himself, the god who has been brought down to earth in the play, and who is in straitened circumstances when it begins: 'It's an absolute outrage that I, Dionysus, son of Juice, have to struggle along on foot.' This translation captures the spirit of the original: the whittling down of 'Zeus' to 'Juice' alludes to the god's association with those who enjoy a tipple, but it also stands as a shorthand for comedy's frequent urge to dethrone gods, to oust father figures, to shake things up a bit. Aristophanes's plays often focus their attentions on the figure of an old man who is magically rejuvenated by defeating his son—a reborn god in his own home, as it were—but they also indulge in other appetites. The chorus leader in *The Birds* (414 BC) tells the audience that fathers are there to be punched: 'put up your spur, if you're fighting'.

This fighting talk calls for new rules. Although anthropological readings of comedy focus on the mode's precursors, the form of what is now termed Old Comedy houses a desire for all things new. Unlike its older, grander sibling Tragedy, comedy started from somewhere close to scratch because comic dramatists were not permitted to recycle plots from myths as tragedians had done. A comic plot is not *mythos*, but *logos* (a word Aristophanes often uses to describe what his plays are up to). In a fragment from *Poesis*, Antiphanes points out that tragedy is 'a cushy art'. Comedians have a much harder task: 'we have to invent everything: new names, setup, action, second act curtain, opening'. This predicament is also an opportunity, and a clearer understanding of Aristophanes's powers of invention can help to clarify the bequest that Old Comedy offered to later ages. The first thing to note about his comic stage is that it's busy, abuzz with motion and exchange. Comedy's chorus, twenty-four people, is twice the size of that required for tragedy. It also takes a liberty which classical tragedy never allows itself: the *parabasis*, in which the chorus turns to address the audience directly, discussing contemporary people and events quite unrelated to the fictional plot. In Aristophanes, these ruptures of theatrical illusion are also frequent outside the *parabasis*, and they announce not only comedy's fascinated interest in the process of its own creativity, but also its hope that the audience members might be somehow in on the act—participators as well as spectators.

These collaborations are offered up as a sensuous temptation. In the *parabasis* of *Wasps* (422 BC), the chorus leader speaks of the playwright himself as an artist who is trying to 'sow a crop of new ideas', and asks that spectators save up his phrases 'like fruit'. This art ripens at those moments when Aristophanes conceives his fertile linguistic imaginings as a microcosm of other kinds of fertility. Plutarch would later complain that the puns were nauseating improprieties, but the playwright's pyrotechnical showmanship (his compounding of elevated and demotic words and his neologisms, as well as his puns) is itself a commitment to the inappropriate. *The Birds*, for example, makes much comic capital out of the fact that the Greek word for 'wing' is a euphemism for 'phallus'. When Tereus says that 'we feed in gardens on white sesame, myrtle berries, poppies and bergamot', he has more than one thing on the tip of his tongue: several of the Greek plant names here allude to female genitalia. This sort of comedy gives people and words time off from business as usual, and it invites its spectators to take pleasure in the ways in which bodies—linguistic or otherwise—may sometimes push their luck.

From the beginning, then, comedy involves a self-conscious appeal to the senses, and to the palpable presence of its audience. The opening of *Frogs* sees Xanthias turn to Dionysus to ask: 'Shall I tell them one of the usual jokes, master, the ones that always get the audience laughing?' This captures the dual rhythm of the comic beginning: although it acknowledges the form's roots in past traditions, it also makes necessity the mother of invention by making new fun out of our need for jokes in the first place. Indeed, jokes, like the larger structures of Old Comedy itself, are both a ritual and a parody of ritual. The anthropologist Mary Douglas sees a joke as 'a play upon form', as a rite and 'an anti-rite'. The pleasure lies in the way that it plays with our sense of what might be allowable: 'the joker as god promises a wealth of new, unforeseeable kinds of interpretation,' she writes, 'a joke implies that anything is possible'. And, perhaps, it also implies that anything can be made to happen simply by expressing the wish for it. In the earliest surviving comedy in the Western canon, Aristophanes's *The Acharnians* (425 BC), Dikaiopolis issues an order to his associate Euripides. The tragedian replies: 'Sorry, it's not possible.' The comedian's response? 'Do it anyway.' In this comic universe, the counterfactual comes good. Comedy sometimes implies that the world will become the world we want—the best of all impossible worlds.

## Country pleasures

A consideration of beginnings can be developed by thinking about *where* as well as *when* comedy starts, and by widening the focus to look at other periods. Attic drama was staged in and for the *polis*, but it was also a way for the city dwellers to reflect critically upon themselves, and upon the appeal of imaginative elsewheres. At the opening of *Birds*, Peisetaerus tells the audience that he's in search of 'a trouble-free place' (the Peloponnesian war had brought trouble to the rural population of Athens, driving many into the city). The hero of *The Acharnians* is Dikaiopolis, meaning 'Honest Citizen', or 'he of the just city'. But he's also a farmer and he begins by grumbling: 'Oh, Athens, Athens, what are you coming to?... I'm gazing at the countryside over yonder... cursing the city and yearning to get back to my village.' It would seem that the goddess of comedy, Thalia (from Greek *Thaleia*, meaning 'luxuriant, blooming' and *thallos*, 'green shoot, twig') presides over an impulse that seeks fruition in some versions of pastoral.

*'In the beginning was the return,'* Maurice Blanchot wrote in 'The Laughter of the Gods'. Many comic beginnings have featured a 'return to nature' of one sort or another: a voyage to Arcadia, or a journey back to a Golden Age, or a search for a lost Eden. Crucially, though, this return to roots is frequently seen as the promise of a *new* beginning—a release from the status quo, or an

escape to freedom. The closing lines of the first Act of Shakespeare's *As You Like It* (*c*.1599) highlight the shift: 'Let's away,' Celia says. 'Now go we in content | To liberty and not to banishment.' Shakespeare's festive comedies partake of the genre's long-standing ambitions to offer us a topography of the mind's most cherished imaginings. In some ways they echo the medieval ritual plays that sought a way for man to absorb the burgeoning energy of the natural world, sharing in what the critic Northrop Frye has called comedy's Mythos of Spring: 'a rhythmic movement from normal world to green world and back again...The green world has analogies, not only to the fertile world of ritual, but to the dream world that we create out of our own desires.' If this world makes us laugh, it is often a joyful, celebratory laughter, one that signals a release from worry. And this release is not merely an escape from reality, but a replenishment of it, as when Rosalind cajoles Orlando among the trees: 'Come woo me, woo me, for now I am in a holiday humour, and like enough to consent.' Her 'now' acknowledges that the mood may not be lasting, yet while it does last it can be a catalyst for things that will survive beyond it.

Shakespeare's comedies are steeped in a rich, diverse heritage of country merriments and holiday customs, including the saturnalia, the carnival, May games, and the election of the Lord of Misrule on Twelfth Night. Some post-Reformation commentators were not amused. The Puritan Phillip Stubbes wrote an *Anatomie of Abuses* (1583), denouncing 'maids going to the wood over-night' and other festivities encouraging 'heathenry, devilry, whoredom, drunkenness, pride and what not'. But comedy enjoys the what not, and *A Midsummer Night's Dream* (*c*.1590–6) leaves us in no doubt about where the trouble starts. It's set in one of the birthplaces of comedy, Athens, but also at a slight remove from the centre: 'in the wood, a league without the town'. The lovers aren't the only ones who seek out the wood; Bottom's troop of actors also go there to rehearse their play, and Shakespeare's comedy here accentuates a link between amorous and literary creativity. As in Aristophanes, the punning energies of the dramatist's language take off in the green world and seem to be in cahoots with the characters' own feelings. When Demetrius says 'And here am I, and wood within this wood,' he means that he is being driven mad with anger ('wood' from the Old English *wód*, meaning 'raging, frantic'), but also that he is being wooed, absorbing the spirit of a place where linguistic and physical bodies are given room to experiment. In *Love's Labour's Lost* (*c*.1590s), Berowne admits: 'I do love, and it hath taught me to rhyme.' Fittingly, the play enjoys the serendipity of one rhyme which stands as testament to comedy's relish for new beginnings: 'mirth/birth'. Often in Shakespeare, when people share a joke they rhyme with each other. It is significant that in *A Midsummer Night's Dream*, once the spell is broken and the lovers leave the wood behind, they never again speak in rhyme.

The idea that comedy should begin by conceiving and searching out the green place has been an enduring one, even when it has proved difficult to get out of the city. Restoration comedy translated the topos into a movement from the town-house interior to the unguarded frisson of the park. The title of William Wycherley's *Love in a Wood, or St James's Park* (1671) marks the transition, and Rochester's 'A Ramble in St James's Park' (*c*.1680) notes that the trees provide ambiguous cover: 'And nightly now beneath their shade | Are Buggeries, Rapes and Incests made.' This is a reminder that comedy's Edens and Ardens can be shadowed by risk. If comic openings often contain drives towards make-believe and wish-fulfilment, the mode's longevity also owes much to its willingness to question these flights of fancy. The self-consciousness of the comic imagination has on many occasions led it to make comedy out of its own deepest yearnings. We might say that the very human need for the joyful laughter of the green world is made laughable.

The idea that the desire for a new beginning can itself be a comic subject is lovingly run through its paces in Gustave Flaubert's *Bouvard and Pécuchet* (1881). 'How good would it be to be in the

13

country!' The novel begins by flourishing its comic credentials as two Parisian copy-clerks strike up a friendship through their desire to be somewhere other than where they are. As soon as Bouvard inherits a fortune, the pair purchase a rural estate, move in, and immediately turn their attentions to the garden. Pécuchet creates 'three compartments, for making composts which would make a lot of things grow, whose waste matters would bring along other crops, supplying further fertilizer, and so on indefinitely... [H]e decided to go out "on the dung-hunt"'. These home economies echo ritual and folklore by reworking the ancient comic rhythm of rebirth from death; as the literary critic and theorist Mikhail Bakhtin observed in his groundbreaking study of Rabelais, 'the language of excrement was closely linked with fertility... defecation and degradation digs a bodily grave for a new birth'. However, as Flaubert's novel proceeds, cravings for abundance become part of the delightfully barren absurdity of the situation. The pair read mountains of books, devise dozens of experiments for domestic improvements, and make increasingly fruitless attempts to keep their dream idyll from turning into a nightmare. If this was meant to be a return to an updated garden of Eden, the Tree of Comic Knowledge in their back garden offers an unexpected lesson. 'Perhaps,' Pécuchet wonders, 'Perhaps arboriculture is just a joke!'

## Trouble in paradise

Comedy involves the construction of a creation myth you can live with. Comic dreamers are often trying to find a way to go back in order to go forward. Yet Bouvard and Pécuchet's geological and religious investigations don't exactly go to plan and they finally decide to resume life as copyists. The joke at the heart of Flaubert's book, one at the heart of many plots which flirt with comedy, is that trying to get back to a Golden Age or an Eden is funny because even when we were there we wanted something else. Samuel Johnson's *The History of Rasselas, Prince of Abyssinia* (1759) begins in the edenic hell on earth that is the Happy Valley, where every conceivable pleasure is available on tap. Rasselas is unimpressed: 'That I want nothing, or that I know not what I want, is the cause of my complaint...I have already enjoyed too much: give me something to desire.' An updated version of this enduringly comic predicament appears in the Talking Heads song, '(Nothing But) Flowers' (1987), which begins at the obligatory beginning—'Here we stand | Like an Adam and an Eve | Water-falls | The Garden of Eden'—before mournfully recalling how much better things used to be:

> There was a shopping mall,
>
> Now it's all covered with flowers...
>
> If this is paradise
>
> I wish I had a lawnmower...
>
> This was a Pizza Hut,
>
> Now it's all covered with daisies...
>
> We used to microwave,
>
> Now we just eat nuts and berries.

If there was a forbidden apple here, they'd scoff it immediately. The song ends with a plea: 'Don't leave me stranded here | I can't get used to this lifestyle.' This lets us in on one of the secrets of the comic way of being in the world: it is so often conceiving, so often in love with the possibility of living many lives, that there is no lifestyle it could ever happily get used to. Comedy may start with a yearning for 'the green place', but it is also an appreciation of the fact that—for those with imagination or with time to kill—the grass is always greener on the other side. The poet-critic Randall Jarrell put it well: 'In a golden age, people go around complaining how yellow everything looks.'

Comedy can make us feel as though the joke is on us. Its double-binds may puncture as well as sustain illusion, and the genre's provocations have frequently led to trouble offstage. When, for example, John Middleton Synge was called to take his part in a new beginning for Irish drama, he turned to comic rhythms as a way of investigating what this particular golden age was meant to be. *The Playboy of the Western World* was first performed in January 1907; Synge's preface spoke against 'the modern literature of towns' and 'places where the springtime of the local life has been forgotten'. So the play's action is another version of the Mythos of Spring and revolves around some central comic tropes. But local life isn't a cosy affair. The playboy Christy Mahon is a rebel against the peasant custom of arranged marriage, a slayer of the father and his law—as his sweetheart Pegeen says: 'you a fine lad with the great savagery to destroy your da'. One critic observed that the play could be seen as a variation on Baudelaire's practical joke, in which the poet enters a Paris restaurant loudly exclaiming: 'After having murdered my poor father…'. This is the quintessential comic opening, delivered with gusto by an Oedipus without the complex.

Aristophanes's audience would have smiled. In comedy, the death of the father-god is usually the prelude to his rebirth, and Christy's father will indeed rise again at the end of the play. Many of Synge's audience, though, were outraged by what they saw as an unflattering portrait of Irish peasant life—too promiscuous by half—deeming the play an insult to Irish womanhood and a slur on the nation. There was rioting in the streets of Dublin. A few nights later, when one of the play's performers reached the line 'There will be right sport before night will fall,' a press reporter noted that 'This was so very apropos to the exciting situation that all parties in the theatre joined in an outburst of hearty laughter.' Hearty, yes, but uneasy too. The 'outburst' here is a reminder that comedy has frequently delighted in stirring up feelings which prove hard to control. If the genre feeds off *komos*, it can also edge towards chaos; revel may become riot. Synge's play is, amongst other things, a critique of the need for a certain kind of nationalist creation story. In his hands, comedy aims to shape the beginning of a new consciousness by giving audiences more than they bargained for.

Comedy still continues to make some of its most promising opening gambits through reshapings of the familiar. The film *Withnail and I* (1987) starts with a need to get outdoors: 'I feel unusual. I think we should go outside,' Withnail suggests to Marwood. We next see them sitting on a bench in Regent's Park—site of many a Restoration comedy—before Marwood has a bright idea: 'Get into the countryside, rejuvenate.' 'Rejuvenate?' Withnail spits, 'I'm in a park and I'm practically dead.' And so begins the overture towards the *urbs in rure*. As the boys leave town, the soundtrack plays the first lines of Hendrix's version of Dylan's 'All Along The Watchtower': '"There must be some way out of here," said the joker to the thief.' From Aristophanes onwards, comic jokers often begin with riffs on this escape artistry. It should be noted, though, that the seeds of country pleasures are already being planted in the city by Withnail's gay uncle, Monty, whose love of sherry and root vegetables draws teasingly on comedy's Dionysian roots, and on ancient vegetation rites as a source of regeneration. When Monty joins his boys in the Lake District, Withnail complains about the food: 'Vegetables again. I'll be sprouting bloody feelers soon.' But the presiding master of ceremonies is insistent: 'Come along. He's going to revitalize himself, and you're going to finish the vegetables.' By the time Monty whispers his sweet nothings to Marwood—'I think we'd better release you from the légumes ... and transfer your talents to the meat'—everyone understands the kind of revitalization he has in mind. In this comedy, as in many others before it, a hankering after meat and two veg survives incognito in other appetites.

The delectable ballet of pun and double entendre is played out across the film, and is the means for its most intrepid, sensitive explorations. *Withnail and I* is largely preoccupied by drink and sexual deviance, with the pair apparently searching for the former and avoiding the latter. Yet when the couple so frequently express a desire to be 'arse-holed', the comedy speaks through them to suggest that maybe what they most fear is what they most want—or most want to understand about themselves. Similarly with their trip to the country. Withnail is adamant that 'We've gone on holiday by mistake,' but the man he says this to is a farmer who has recently been gored by 'a randy bull'. Withnail's line is a great one (he's made a joke 'by mistake', we could say) and perhaps it unwittingly speaks volumes about what he's really after. If many comedies are comedies of errors, it might also be ventured that, in this universe, a mistake is often something you secretly want to make.

Bruce Robinson, the writer and director of the film, once said that Huysmans's *À Rebours* (1884) was the funniest book he'd ever read. This is the novel we catch a glimpse of Marwood packing in his suitcase as he leaves Withnail at the end of the film, and it's the comedy's quiet way of confessing that it will take its beginnings with it even as it moves on to other, apparently more serious occupations. Huysmans said that his novel had 'a pinch of dark humour and dry English comedy'. The hero, Des Esseintes, is a prototype for Withnail—a dark, dry dandy of sorts, staging and upstaging his own contradictory desires as a way of enjoying and enduring them. Comedy characteristically begins with desire before encouraging us to laugh at it, but—in doing so—it can also reconcile us *to* desire, make it somehow easier to live with. This informing impulse is captured brilliantly when Withnail bawls out at the top of his voice in the middle of the Lake District: 'Bastards! I'll show the lot of you... I'm going to be a star!' As he drags the 'star' out of 'bastard', he is indulging in yet another version of the comic dream, a dream which insists upon its right to make up new beginnings in the most unpromising circumstances. What we are enjoying here is the birth of another fractious star.

# Chapter 2
## **Getting physical**

'No,' I said, 'this is comedy,' and threw the biscotti—and his skinny mocha latte—right back in his face. Edgy, humourless F, 41, banned from most train-station Costas. Strangely alone at box. no. 6323.

Personal ad, *London Review of Books*

## Minding the body

Although comedy eludes precise definition, one of its recurring effects is tangible enough—what Descartes called 'the inarticulate and explosive cry…laughter'. If only that cry could speak clearly. Then it could be ascertained where it comes from, and what it means. Is it civilized or savage? High or low? In *The Anatomy and Philosophy of Expression* (1824), Charles Bell noted that, during laughter, the lower part of the face obtrudes upon the upper, 'the eye is especially diminutive…the face loses all dignity and form'. Yet, as the physician Guillaume-Benjamin Duchenne pointed out in *The Mechanism of Human Facial Expression* (1862), wholehearted laughter begins with the eyes, mobilizing the *orbicularis oculi* muscle as well as the muscles around the mouth. Going along with the spirit of the game as played by Duchenne, it might be suggested that, during a laugh, the upper part of the face raises the lower rather than being engulfed by it. Laughter could be seen not as the 'loss' but as the finessing of form. A laugh is an achievement. In *The Expression of the Emotions in Man and Animals* (1872), Charles Darwin confessed that the causes of laughter were obscure, but—turning from the seen to the heard—noted that 'throughout a large part of the animal kingdom vocal or instrumental sounds are employed either as a call or as a charm by one sex for the other'. Highly evolved behaviour, then, in the service of our most primitive needs? The allegedly humourless female who wrote that personal ad knows a thing or two about comedy: her recounted act was aggressive, but her recounting of the act may be something akin to a mating cry.

In the Aristotelian tradition, man is the laughing animal. Or, rather, he is distinguished from the animals by the fact that he *can* laugh. *Homo ridens* is the thinking man. The novelist and activist Arthur Koestler argued that 'laughter rings the bell of man's departure from the rails of his instinct; it signals his rebellion against the single-mindedness of his biological urges'. But Koestler's metaphor here spells trouble for his theory; going off the rails usually suggests not so much a departure from urges and instincts as a furtherance of them. Max Beerbohm felt that something less straightforwardly cerebral was going on during a good laugh: 'the emotion of laughter is partly physical, partly mental'. If laughter is a halfway house, then it may signal man's awareness of himself as a strange medley of the physical and the mental. Simon Critchley has argued that this very awareness is a vital aspect of much humour. On one level, a person *is* their body, but he or she can also reflect—as most animals seemingly cannot—on the idea of *having* a body, and on the idea that selfhood is not wholly defined by the physical self. This chapter thinks about comedy as a mode through which we organize our knowledge of ourselves as material beings who can revel in and cast aspersions on our own materiality. From Aristophanes onwards, comic imaginations have enjoyed getting physical, but part of that enjoyment is bound up in thinking *about* the physical. From this perspective, comedy encourages a double-take, an oscillating rhythm of immersion and distance. When cracking up, being 'beside ourselves', or doubling up with laughter, we arrive at a heightened awareness of ourselves as oddly plural.

Comic figures and modes frequently gesture towards bodily appetites—and perhaps towards one sense of the gender of comedy. The phallus was always onstage in Greek comedy, and the wine-swilling, sexually voracious satyr—an animal-like man and companion of Dionysus—is the first of many performers who like to flaunt what they've got (Howard Jacobson has listed many other family members: Harlequin's *batte*, Punch's cudgel, the jester's *marotte*, Chaplin's cane, and Ken Dodd's tickling stick). Not that comedy is an exclusively male preserve—Lisa Lampanelli gives that old line short shrift: 'You know, if "funny" is a guy-thing, then I'll strap it on.' From Dorothy Parker to *Ab Fab* and beyond, many jokes have been made with and at the tickling stick. Sarah Silverman's stand-up usually involves occasion for thinking about the penis as a source of pleasure and horror ('A couple nights ago, I was licking jelly off my boyfriend's penis. And I thought, "Oh my god, I'm turning into my mother!"'). Bodies caught in the act thinking—this is a paradoxical and primal comic scene. In his *School for Aesthetics* (1804), Jean Paul Richter argued that 'the comic cannot exist without sensuousness'; the comic writer 'fastens our mind upon physical detail'. This focus has often led comedy to the borders of transgression and taboo. An enduring mode of English humour depicts lives preoccupied by sensuousness, and it finds its ripest early expression in Geoffrey Chaucer's relish for the telling physical detail.

In the Prologue of the *Canterbury Tales* (*c.*1390s), we learn of the Franklin that 'Of his complexioun he was sangwin; | Well loved he by the morwe a sop in win' ('by the morwe': 'in the morning'). The first line alludes to the medieval medical theory of the four humours, so 'sangwin' picks up on the Franklin's ruddy colouring as well as his cheerful disposition. The second line is a dab of local colour (bread dipped in wine was a standard medieval breakfast), but it also hints at an unholy communion of sorts, fitting for a pilgrim who has more than religious matters in mind. Frequently in Chaucer's writing there's a feeling for the tangible as the incarnation of a more generalized state of affairs. The Wife of Bath has 'on hir feet a peire of spores sharpe. | In felawshipe wel koude she laughe and carpe.' The spurs seem to transfer a kind of glinting light to her laughing, carping mouth. Her laugh is a show of teeth. She has bite as well as gusto, and is more than happy to make an ass of the male of the species—five husbands and counting...

From the coxcomb of the fool to the horns of the cuckold, man's animality is rife in comedy. Chaucer's tales make humans laughable by drawing out the beast within (one of the poet's favourite rhymes is 'ape'|'jape'). In 'The Miller's Tale', the miller's wife Alison is described within the space of a few lines as a weasel, a kid, a swallow, a calf, and a colt. These details prime both the reader and the wily young clerk for beastly pleasures, and as soon as the husband pops out, 'As clerkes been ful subtil and ful queinte | And prively he caughte hire by the queinte.' As adjective, 'queinte' means 'clever or subtle'; as noun, there is some scholarly debate about whether to translate it as 'cunt' or 'crotch', but the point is clear enough. The pun is in league with the broader comic energies of the story. It encourages awareness of the physical desire which drives mental agility. In 'The Shipman's Tale', the unfaithful wife has the audacity to suggest paying off her infidelity through sexual favours: 'if so be I faille, | I am youre wif, score it upon my taille.' 'Taille' is slang for 'arse, genitals', but it's also a 'tally', a scored stick kept by a creditor as a record of sums owing, so the wife may or may not be about to kiss and make up. A few lines later, the narrator consummates his story: 'Thus endeth my tale, and God us send | Tailling inough unto our lives ende!' So 'tailling' is verbal as well as sexual—Chaucer's tales are themselves tails. In this comic territory, it seems, there is more than one way to get your end away. Chaucer's appetite for the pun is a way of exploring what Critchley has described as 'the *physical* and *metaphysical* aspects of being human'. The pun keeps the body in mind by suggesting that the mind's operations are themselves tangled up in bodily matters.

Comedy takes notice of the fact that—again, unlike most animals—humans enjoy their appetites not as necessities, but as luxuries (the liaisons in *The Canterbury Tales* are sought more for recreation than procreation). The human animal, it might be ventured, makes *too much* of appetite, so comedy offers a chance to reflect on this odd side of ourselves. The same goes for those who do not eat to live, but who live to eat. If you can stomach a joke, or indulge in belly laughs, then you probably also have a taste for comic forms: lampoon (from the French *lampons*, 'let us drink'); pastiche (from the Italian *pasticcio*, 'any manner of pastie or pye'); satire (from the Latin *satura*, elliptical for *lanx satura*, meaning 'full dish'—a dish 'for food composed of many different ingredients' (*OED*)). The fullest of dishes is to be found in the work of the Renaissance writer François Rabelais. In his comic 'Chronicles' (1532–64), the giants Gargantua, Pantagruel, and their associates gobble and guzzle their way through one thousand and one pages. One of the author's greatest creations, Friar John, introduces himself by expressing concern about the abbey's vineyard: 'By the guts of Saint James, what shall we poor devils be drinking in the meantime? Lord God, *Give me a drink*.' 'Da mihi potum' ('Give me a drink') is a monastic joke, sometimes written by tired scribes at the end of a manuscript, so this is Rabelais's way of telling us that, in comedy, the writer and his characters are not inclined to wait. As Withnail will insist much later in *Withnail and I*: 'We want the finest wines available to humanity, and we want them *here*, and we want them *now*.'

These voices are reminders that the comic body is often copious. It's the body impolitic—ravenous, demanding, embarrassing. Mikhail Bakhtin imagines it as a grotesque image, 'looking for that which protrudes from the body, all that seeks to go out beyond the body's confines'. The all-engulfing figure here is the mouth, the body part that Bakhtin sees as the hero of Rabelais's book. Indeed, the Chronicles were conceived and written in a drought, and its protagonist Pantagruel (from *pan*, 'all' and *gruel*, 'thirst') has an appetite so large that at one point he consumes his narrator. A body this open ended is usually open at both ends. Like his maker, Pantagruel is philosophical and visceral—'deep in thought . . . and farting under the strain'. His reading matter keeps him grounded, and makes even flatulence seem fruitful: titles include *On the Art of Discreetly Farting in Company*, *The Abbots' Ass-pizzles*, and *Bum-volleys of Papal Bullists*.

Toilet humour abounds. The book is lavishly besmeared and drenched in shit and piss, with the motions of the soul affecting those of the bowels ('Madam, you should know that I am so deeply in love with you that I can neither piddle nor pooh'). This scatological energy is a frequent presence in comedy, a vital part of the mode's fascination with the human being as a site of competing impulses. C. S. Lewis suggested that 'the coarse joke proclaims that we have here an animal which finds its own animality either objectionable or funny. Unless there had been a quarrel between the spirit and the organism I do not see how this could be: it is the very mark of the two not being "at home" together.' To which it might be replied that the coarse joke is also a way for the spirit and the organism to make up, or at least to live with each other (even if not feeling wholly 'at home'). Our animality is objectionable *and* funny; in finding it funny we somehow make it slightly less objectionable. After all, every household needs to budget for the toilet as well as the toilette.

## 'The physique of our pleasures'

Prose like Rabelais's asks you—dares you—to read it aloud. It wants its reader to join the celebration of the mouth, to luxuriate in the verbal fluency, filth, and fireworks. 'Humour, I suspect, is an oral genre,' Jorge Luis Borges suggested, 'a sudden flavour of conversation, not written.' Perhaps this is why comedy tends so often to seek expression in stage drama. Theatre is the art of bodies speaking and moving in enclosed spaces, so it is hospitable to comedy's long-standing interest in what might be done within the realm of the physical. Indeed, Restoration drama of the late 17th century explored the pleasures and perils of the flesh by bringing a new body on stage. Breaking with the convention of boy-actors playing female roles, in 1660 a professional English actress appeared on the English public stage for the first time. The figure of the actress had a shady reputation—she was often seen as a prostitute or a kept mistress—but she also asked delicate questions of her well-heeled spectators in the auditorium.

In William Wycherley's *The Country Wife* (1675), the wife is looking for trouble and demands that her husband take her to see a play. Having been to the theatre, however, she complains: 'Ay, but we sat amongst ugly people; he would not let me come near the gentry, who sat under us, so that I could not see 'em. He told me none but naughty women sat there, whom they toused and moused.' This feels like 'a sudden flavour of conversation', a way for Wycherley's play and his player to draw attention to the audience's implication in the vice it laughs at on stage. The upper-class men and women are not to be dissociated from the rakes and loose women they observe; as Horner points out to Lady Fidget, 'your virtue is your greatest affectation, madam'. Aphra Behn's *The Rover* (1677) sees another young heroine, Helena, begin by confessing that 'I love mischief strangely, as most of our sex do who are come to love nothing else.' 'Come to'? A good actress will use her body—the inflections of her voice and her gestures—to hint that 'come to' means not just 'this is what becomes of people like me', but also 'you too, ladies, who today are come to watch this play'. When the libertine Willmore cries 'Damn propriety!' he also means to damn those who fake propriety. 'I have lain with a woman of quality who has all the while been railing at whores,' he notes, with one eye on those seated or reclining in the audience.

Restoration comedy is about what the body wants in relation to what people say they want. It explores the tension between sexual desire and social demands by making sure the members of the audience never forget that their own bodies are referred to and involved in the onstage spectacle. If there is a single image, though, which this kind of drama excels in—and through which it concentrates its exploration of the tussle between head and heart—it's the one George Meredith saw as the ideal comic situation: the picture of the affectionate couple quarrelling. In Congreve's *The Way of The World* (1700), Mirabell ventures, 'You are merry, madam, but I would persuade you for one moment to be serious,' to which Millamant replies, 'What, with that face? . . . Well, after all, there is something very moving in a love-sick face. Ha! ha! ha!—Well, I won't laugh.' She laughs and she won't laugh. Fighting is flirting. A brush-off is a come-on. The rhythm is a recurring one in comedy (from Shakespeare's Beatrice and Benedict to Jane Austen's Elizabeth and Darcy and beyond). Being in love is itself a comic double act. The couple rely on wit to gain some mastery over feelings that they cannot quite control.

As he reflects on how people's affections are subject to change, Mirabell observes: 'To know this, and yet continue to be in love, is to be made wise from the dictates of reason, and yet persevere to play the fool by the force of instinct.' Pondering the limits of reason in this way is a bass note of Restoration drama, and it's another version of comedy's long-standing interest in negotiations between mind and body. This comedy is often located at the intersection between the discourses of wit and humour. Wit (from *witan*, 'to know') is a kind of cognitive prowess or psychological cunning, whereas humour (from *humorem*, 'fluid, moisture', hence the four bodily humours) is perhaps more aligned with feeling, mood, physiology. When Thackeray defined 'humour' as 'wit and love', he was offering support for the idea of a romantic comedy that could speak to each side of the mental–physical divide. The image of the affectionate couple quarrelling might be translated into the following equation: wit + love = keeping your head + being head over heels.

So comedy frequently involves a play between physical and cognitive perspectives. This is why comic energies are often heightened through expression which itself revels in a dialogue between the sensory and cerebral elements of language. The figure of rhyme, for example, allows poets not only to employ words as conceptual counters, but to play around with them as physical bodies—to enjoy them for their sound, their shape, their acoustic contours. The figure proves especially promising for lovers of comic and corporeal misadventure, as Byron appreciates in *Don Juan* (1819–24), where the narrator enjoys his rhymes like he enjoys his lovers—frequent, flirtatious, unruly. Not that such appetites are without complications: '"Kiss" rhymes to "bliss" in fact as well as verse— | I wish it never led to something worse.' A comic rhyme will relish an appeal to the body, whilst also acknowledging that bodies, like rhymes, may lead you to places you hadn't initially planned to go.

*Don Juan* illustrates comedy's willingness to entertain the idea of man as reasonable and risible. Byron's rhyming gambits are a central part of this drama; they present the image of a person being awkwardly stationed between being a mind that acts on a body, and a body that seems to have a mind of its own. When Juan turns philosopher by pondering 'the boundless skies' alongside the look in 'Donna Julia's eyes', the narrator turns to the reader: 'If *you* think 'twas philosophy that this did, | I can't help thinking puberty assisted.' Later, Juan and Julia try to stay virtuous (Julia is a married woman) by not giving in to temptation:

> And Julia's voice was lost, except in sighs,
> Until too late for useful conversation;
> The tears were gushing from her gentle eyes,
> I wish, indeed, they had not had occasion,
> But who, alas! can love, and then be wise?
> Not that remorse did not oppose temptation,
> A little still she strove, and much repented,
> And whispering 'I will ne'er consent'—consented.

Rhyming couplets often provide occasion for coupling up in *Don Juan*. As readers, we want this rhyme to be consummated, to hear the sound of linguistic bodies coming together, and our expectancy is not to be entirely dissociated from Julia's. In some sense we are partner to her crime. But there's an extra twist in 'repented/consented', for doesn't one normally repent of an act *after* one has done it? Julia's mind is already dealing with the consequences of an act her body has not yet undertaken, which makes the repentance itself something less than wholehearted. Fittingly, given his interests, the *OED* credits Byron with the first use of the word 'physique' in English: 'It seems strange,' he says, 'a true voluptuary will never abandon his mind to the grossness of reality. It is by exalting the earthly, the material, the *physique* of our pleasures... that we alone can prevent them from disgusting.' There is a rueful, self-knowing comedy in this insight, one that Donna Julia would perhaps appreciate. The true voluptuary is a kind of idealist. He or she commits to bodily pleasures (as opposed to merely indulging in them) by acknowledging that these pleasures are a mixed blessing: exalted *and* earthly. In comedy, the moment you are most like an animal is also a moment in which you will find a way to understand yourself as more than that.

## Jest and gesture

'Julia's voice was lost.' Comic forms are often on the lookout for those moments in which actions speak louder than words, or where physical gesture runs up against mental resolutions. The word 'jest' itself comes from Old French (*geste, jeste*), meaning 'action, exploit', and a modern version of this teasing combination is the sight gag—the voiceless, gesture-rich world of silent film comedy, especially that of Charlie Chaplin and Buster Keaton. Eugene Ionesco cannily suggested: 'If you want to turn tragedy into comedy, speed it up.' Early slapstick cinema teases out the physical implications of this idea; it presents us with bodies that fall, without completely falling foul. Cameras were hand-cranked, so films were shot at 16 or 18 frames per second, but then projected at a quicker speed, something close to sound-projection rate. The result is faster than life—and, strangely, *safer* than life. These bodies are usually in danger (from falling buildings, moving vehicles, swinging fists), yet also astonishingly resilient, quickly back on their feet, and up for more. And while bodily unruliness sabotages the best-laid plans of the mind, another paradox emerges: although the fictional character's body loses control, this is a *staged* loss of control in the actor's body, a staging which itself requires outstanding mental and physical agility. The pleasures of slapstick come from the sight of the human being as at once beholden and resistant to the demands of the body. What we encounter here is not quite an image of mind over matter, but of mind minding matter.

Chaplin's achievement can be usefully approached via two modern theories of the comic. The philosopher Henri Bergson sensed comedy whenever we see the human turning mechanical: '*The attitudes, gestures, and movements of the human body,*' he stressed, '*are laughable in exact proportion as that body reminds us of a mere machine.*' For Wyndham Lewis, though, humans *are* mechanical. What's really funny is seeing mechanical things aspire to be something above their station: 'The root of the Comic is to be sought in the sensation resulting from the observations of a *thing* behaving like a person. But from that point of view all men are necessarily comic: for they are all *things*, or physical bodies, behaving as *persons.*'

In Chaplin's early masterpiece, *The Pawnshop* (1916), the joke initially revolves around Charlie inspecting a customer's clock as if it were a person (listening for a heartbeat, performing surgery on its internal organs), but then, suddenly, the clock's insides do come to life and start moving of their own accord on the counter (see Figure 2). The clock is not just behaving *like* a person, but shedding light on what a person might be: an assemblage of body parts with a will of their own. When Chaplin finally sees fit to hit the unsatisfied customer with a hammer (just as he had earlier hit

2. Charlie Chaplin, *The Pawnshop* (1916)

the clock), it's not so much an act of violence, but rather as though he's trying to correct a malfunction. The customer is a thing behaving like a person—how very odd.

If Chaplin bends the physical universe to his will, Keaton lets the universe happen to him and yet somehow emerges from the encounter unscathed. Nobody ever made the act of going through the motions—or of just sitting still—more comically and humanly compelling. After his lady-love has spurned him in *The General* (1927), Johnnie sits on the driving-bar of his locomotive. 'What's the point of going on?' his slouch seems to say (see Figure 3).

Johnnie is so disconsolate that he isn't even aware that the engine has started. As the train moves forward, the driving-bars carry him along in a series of exquisite arcs (the effect has to be seen to be believed). The train is sympathizing with him, gently cradling him in its arms. A machine turns personable just at the

**3. Buster Keaton, *The General* (1927)**
(To view this: http://youtu.be/aM1aiXGxmts)

moment when a person feels drained of life. Motionless yet on the move, Keaton cuts a ruefully comic figure. The train lends his body a gently buoyant mood which he isn't currently feeling. In doing so, it prompts his mind to come to its senses.

In Keaton's films, trapdoors become escape hatches, mishaps are the catalysts for miracles, oversights seem inspired. This is another long-standing comic law: the body will finally come good (or, at least, will come through), provided one doesn't overthink things. Keaton's most famous sight gag sees a building collapse on him during a cyclone, only to reveal that he was in the exactly the right place at the right time (see Figure 4).

The open attic window fits him like a glove. Keaton is the calm at the centre of the storm. This is not to say that his character is 'in control' of the situation, but rather that, according to the rules of this comic universe, he is permitted to observe—and to

31

**4. Buster Keaton, *Steamboat Bill Jr* (1928)**

outlive—the havoc which both surrounds and sustains him. The effect of his posture here is not unlike that of his beautifully deadpan face; it offers tentative protection from the heartache and the thousand natural shocks that flesh is heir to.

Comedy can turn plight into pleasure. It pauses to wonder at the fact that we have to carry our bodies around with us, whilst also allowing us to reconceive them in new ways. Roland Barthes suggests that 'the body is the most imaginary of all imaginary objects'. The comic imagination has on many occasions been sympathetic to this point of view. It encourages fantasies about what bodies might be or do, which is perhaps why our sex lives so often seem to involve or invite laughter. Those placing personal ads frequently demand that prospective suitors have a GSOH, although to say that 'you need a sense of humour to go out with me' may be a confession as well as a demand. But what is the S in a GSOH? A sense of something is knowledge of it ('sense' as cerebral, cultivated), but a sense is also sensory, immediate. Perhaps humour is something like a sixth sense, hovering on the threshold of mental achievement and physical stimulus: you have humorous thoughts as well as a funny bone.

'Did I mention,' Portnoy wonders, 'that when I was fifteen I took it out of my pants and whacked off on the 107 bus from New York?' Well, no, he didn't, but he did mention that he'd fucked his family's dinner a few years back, using a slab of liver to masturbate with before chucking it back in the fridge in time for tea. Philip Roth has stayed interested in how and why comedy gets physical since *Portnoy's Complaint* (1969). His answers to Mark Lawson's questions during an interview on Radio 4 in 2011 are a valuable reminder, though, that the best approach to this kind of humour will acknowledge its very resistance to theorization, its love of contrariness. Under pressure to explain the significance of 'the green dildo' in a scene from *The Humbling* (2009), Roth responded: 'Sometimes a dildo is just a dildo.' Lawson wasn't satisfied, and continued to hunt for 'the meaning' of such scenes, suggesting to Roth that 'you must put a meaning on the book'. But the comic spirit, if not exactly conceptless, is often winningly impatient with concepts. Roth's final word on the matter feels like the right one: 'I tend not to abstract or generalise about the book. I'm involved dildo by dildo.'

# Chapter 3
# In and out of character

> LORD CURRYFIN: I flatter myself, I am a character (*laughing*).
> MISS GRYLL: (*laughing*) Indeed you are, or rather many
> characters in one.
>
> Thomas Love Peacock, *Gryll Grange* (1860)

## Typecasting and role playing

Some people never change. 'There's always time for a drink,'
Withnail says at the end of *Withnail and I*, bottle in hand,
true to type as ever. Henri Bergson claimed that this predictability
is the secret of comedy: 'Every comic character is a *type*.
Inversely, every resemblance to a type has something comic in it.'
Character becomes comic as person is reduced to thing, and this
thing-ness is recognized as something ossified, habitual, or
inflexible, as '*something mechanical encrusted on the living*'. In
this schema, for *mechanical*, read *unconscious*, and for *living*,
read *variable*. According to Bergson, the truly comic figure is
a kind of monomaniac, unaware that he is comic, and laughter
at such figures is issued as a corrective in order to return them to
their humanity. So comic character has a ridiculous kind of
compulsion to repeat: someone has become their own self-parody
through too faithful an adherence to what makes them tick.

This rings true enough in some cases, although it should be noted that Bergson's theory contains an unacknowledged comedy of its own. His repeated claim that '*every* comic character' is rigid bespeaks a rigidity that is mechanically unable to entertain other possibilities (as George Meredith once suggested, 'any intellectual pleading of a doubtful cause contains germs of an idea of comedy'). Certainly, Bergson's approach misses out on the semi-knowing, quizzical side of characters like Withnail. Bergson says that 'life should never repeat itself', but in Italo Svevo's novel *Zeno's Conscience* (1923), Zeno Cosini rightly senses the life *in* repetition, making comedy out of his many attempts to give up smoking: 'That was a very important last cigarette,' he recalls with panache. This last-cigarette routine is more than just another instance of the mechanical encrusted on the living: 'Striking a beautiful attitude, one says: "Never again." But what becomes of that attitude if the promise is then kept? It's possible to strike the attitude only when you are obliged to renew the vow.' Zeno strikes an attitude as a delicious prelude to the striking of a match. He knows that to quit smoking would be to give up on that part of himself which enjoys giving up. The character plays both parts of his own double act, and takes encouragement from the idea that he is not quite equal to himself, nor to his own best intentions. It's not long before he takes to carrying 'a next-to-last cigarette' in his pocket, just to be on the safe side.

Characters like Zeno provide support for G. K. Chesterton's claim that in humour there is 'the idea of the eccentric caught in the act of eccentricity and brazening it out'. So the figure is sharing a joke with himself. Ralph Waldo Emerson suggested that the essence of comedy is 'a well-intentioned halfness ... a non-performance of what is pretended to be performed, at the same time that one is giving loud pledges of performance'. This counterpoint to Bergson's position usefully suggests that a comic character is not just the unwitting dupe of his repetitions. He may, on occasion, be the self-conscious explorer of them. Half trapped and half tongue-in-cheek, he acts and satirizes himself. So two perceptions of comic character compete for attention here, both of which are laughable: the tableau of a frozen, stereotyped self, and the drama of a self which is other than it appears. Artists and writers have gravitated towards each model, and have often sought to combine them. Beckett's *Molloy* offers a droll contribution to the debate: 'One is what one is, partly at least.' Hovering somewhere between personal testimony and grand theory, Molloy's quip can stand as the kernel of this chapter's investigation into how comic characters have been viewed across the ages.

The notion that the stock character is ridiculous has a long heritage. Theophrastus's *Characters* (*c.*319 BC) depicts The Chatterbox, The Penny-Pincher, and many others who live and breathe only one kind of air. Theophrastus takes his bearings from Greek comic drama, in which each actor wore a large, grotesque mask that covered the whole head. The mask can conceal and reveal. It may imply that the complexity of a person has been diluted to a persona, but in a huge amphitheatre (holding perhaps as many as 17,000 spectators) it also enables members of the audience to see which specific part is being played by making the person larger than life. Greek drama also required actors to play several parts, so masks allowed the same actor to switch character between scenes. The mask gestures not just towards typecasting, but also towards role playing.

One of the most influential models of comedy in European culture, the New Comedy of Menander, sees the apotheosis of the stock character (the ardent lover, the irascible father, and so on), but it also brings a more naturalistic, nuanced presentation of character than was on show in Old Comedy. Aristophanes of Byzantium found Menander's portrayal of character so true to life that he was moved to ask: 'Menander and life, which of you imitated which?' This joke is in tune with the dramatist's own engagement with the nature of identity. In the first scene of *Dyskolos* (317–16 BC), the audience is confronted by a stock type—the gallant who has fallen for the girl next door—and Chaireas twits him: 'You fell in love at first sight, Sostratos? That was quick! Or was that your idea when you came out, to fall for a girl?' In other words: desire may get ahead of itself, may be so hungry that any object will do. It persuades the desirer that a stock type is a special individual (*the* girl rather than just 'a girl'). Chaireas's comment raises a central question about comic character: is the young man in the grip of a sincere, heartfelt obsession, or is he so keen to play a role that he's making himself up as he goes along? Perhaps both. Sostratos and Sostratos The Young Lover, which of you imitated which?

Under Menander's deft management, the stock figure takes on a strange, new energy. Character becomes motive as well as motif. The action of Menandrian drama creates ever more vertiginous patterns for the ambiguities we've been considering because, although the plays trade in stereotypes, they are often preoccupied by cases of mistaken identity, unlikely feats of substitution, with all and sundry play-acting at one time or another. Indeed, comedy's choreography of recognition and intrigue sees even straightforward characters become tricky to read. *Samia* (*c*.309 BC) features a moment when Nikeratos is shocked to find his daughter breastfeeding a baby in his house. He explains this to Demeas, a friend who has just been disabused of the notion that his own mistress Chrysis is the baby's mother (Demeas had himself come across Chrysis breastfeeding the child earlier in the play). Demeas now tries to hide the fact that his son got Nikeratos's daughter pregnant. Breastfeeding a baby? Surely not, Demeas ventures. 'Perhaps she was just pretending.' In Menander's universe, you can 'pretend' to do or be just about anything—even simply to be yourself. If this comedy takes its initial cue from the idea of the fixed type, it gains fresh momentum from the idea that character can be dangerously and delightfully provisional.

## Humours, caricatures, costumes

The stage has been particularly hospitable to comedy's interest in the vagaries of identity, not least because the chameleonic figure of the actor is itself a shady character. The word 'hypocrite' comes from the Greek word for 'actor', and the *OED*'s primary definition of the word 'comedian' contains a suggestive ambiguity: 1a. 'one who plays in comedies' and 1b. 'one who acts a feigned part in real life'. So the comic mode exacerbates the duplicity. It confronts audiences not just with an actor playing someone else (this is true of any drama), but also with that character themselves acting up, frequently upsetting any settled sense of who they are. Perhaps 1a. harbours a secret ambition to become 1b. Small wonder, then, that in Congreve's *Love for Love* (1695), Valentine should plead with Angelica: 'the comedy draws toward an end, and let us think of leaving acting and be ourselves'. But by the time the comedy has ended, the lesson seems to have been that character is not something you are, but something you play. Many comedies have been entranced by the image of a person who never quite coincides with themselves, even when that person is at their most single-minded.

This odd person has many incarnations, and the discourse of 'the humours' breathes fresh life into him. The term is derived from ancient and medieval physiology to refer to the four body fluids (blood, phlegm, black bile, and yellow bile) that were said to determine character. In *Every Man Out of His Humour* (1599), Ben Jonson speaks of the process through which 'some one peculiar quality | Doth so possess a man, that it doth draw | All his affects, his spirits, and his powers, | In their confluctions, all to run one way'. The man possessed is fertile comic ground, as Molière understood. An actor as well as a playwright, Molière was a comedian in the full sense of the term, and early on in his career he took many roles in the *commedia dell'arte*. This form of theatre relied heavily on stock characters and asked actors to play in masks. But while the mask fixed the character, it freed the actor. There were very few written parts, so actors had to improvise the action and their lines. So the person was pre-scripted and unscripted. At once obsessive and histrionic, this figure was a vital influence on Molière's contribution to the art of comic character building.

As the title suggests, *The Misanthrope* (1666) paints the portrait of a type, but what Molière saw was that the very need to imagine oneself *as* a type can signal a kind of evasion. The misanthropic Alceste (played by Molière himself) enacts a 'personage' in order to avoid his own personality. So concerned is he by what society says and thinks, he erects a defence to shield himself from this concern. The woman he falls for—Célimène, first played by Molière's wife—has got his number, though:

> Don't you see, he must be opposed to you?
> Would you have him accept the common view,
> And not display, in every company,
> His heaven-sent gift for being contrary?

Contrariness looks antisocial, but it bears the stamp of a vanity which is deeply social; this is why Alceste needs to 'display' his opposition. Like many of Molière's protagonists, he wants to make a spectacle of himself, playing up to the environment he shuns. The same goes for Molière's *Don Juan* (1665); after the protagonist makes an apparently heartfelt speech in defence of promiscuity, Sganarelle chips in: 'It seems as though you've learned it by heart, and you talk just like a book.' A so-called 'character trait' may be a covert expression of its opposite. As a pose learnt by rote, the trait itself may become the mask.

Molière's achievement is informed by his understanding of how comedy is frequently born from the disparity between what a person is and what he affects to be. That said, the society and the audience which ridicule such figures are not immune to the disease. Alceste's reply to Célimène's speech above is: 'The laughers are with you, Madame; you've won. | Go on and satirize me; have your fun.' The oh-so-polished members of the anti-misanthropic brigade—those who praise politeness, discretion, 'getting along'—are not just Alceste's foil, but also his double, for they too affect to be something they are not, playing roles because they care so much about the views of the

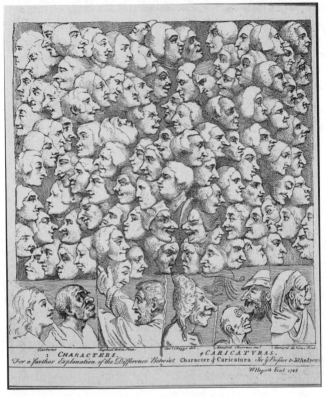

5. William Hogarth, *Characters and Caricaturas* (1743)

in-crowd. Etiquette covers for expediency. In Molière's work, to be 'with' the laughers is not a wholly comforting experience; jokes rebound on the jokers.

The playwright's interest in an extreme yet eerily familiar form of 'the type' is part of comedy's long flirtation with the idea that you can reveal the truth about people by stretching it. The painter Annibale Carracci wrote that 'A good caricature, like every work of art, is more true to life than reality itself', and caricature is a stopping place en route to the shaping of comic character. William Hogarth's visions of reality are chock-full of stock types from comic drama—harlots, rakes, cuckolds—but he was careful to distinguish his work on 'character' from that of caricature (see Figure 5).

The bottom of this etching refers us to Henry Fielding's preface to *Joseph Andrews* (1742), where Hogarth is praised as a 'Comic History-Painter' and distinguished from those caricaturists who seek to go beyond 'the exactest Copy of Nature'. The distinction is important, yet one thing that makes Hogarth's work so provocative is his attraction to depicting characters who seem to be living their lives as a kind of deformed and distorted art. In Hogarth's work there is, in William Hazlitt's superb phrase, 'a tilt and tournament of absurdities': 'his faces go to the very verge of caricature, and yet never go beyond it'. At least two such faces feature in this denouement (see Figure 6).

**6.** *The Bagnio*, from *Marriage-à-la-Mode* (1743–5)

The painting reads like a burlesque of *commedia dell'arte*. Husband bursts in to find Wife with Lover; Lover stabs Husband [*exit Lover through window stage-right*]; Wife falls on one knee before Husband; Husband swoons in slow motion (something akin to Bottom playing Pyramus—'Thus die I, | Thus, thus, thus, | Now am I dead'); [*enter Constable and Proprietor in night-cap stage-left*]. Yet there is horror here too, a sense that the protagonists have made a mess and a caricature out of their own lives, lost sight of themselves by becoming prisoners of the roles they were playing. For Hogarth, as for Molière, the depiction of comic characters often seems to throw up a perplexed ambiguity about whether they should be read as agents or victims.

At the foot of Hogarth's scene lie the accoutrements of a night at the masquerade (costumes and masks clutter the floor). The artist's first self-published print was on *Masquerades and Operas* (1724), and many other writers and artists have since been drawn to the masquerade as an emblem of a culture that is laughable because it has been so easily seduced by duplicity. Samuel Johnson bemoaned the way that 'the rich and powerful live in a perpetual masquerade, in which all about them wear borrowed characters', while Oliver Goldsmith's epilogue to Charlotte Lennox's play *The Sister* (1769) turns on the audience in the boxes, pit, and gallery: 'The world's a masquerade! the maskers, you, you, you.' Comedy's own attraction to 'borrowed characters' renders these satirical thrusts double-edged. In Goldsmith's *She Stoops to Conquer* (1773), Marlow whispers a knowing aside to the audience about Mr Hardcastle: 'A very impudent fellow, this! But he's a character, and I'll humour him a little.' This is the *OED*'s first citation of *character* meaning 'an odd, extraordinary or eccentric person', but what Marlow doesn't know is that he is *mis*reading character; he thinks Mr Hardcastle is an innkeeper getting above his station, rather than the owner of a country estate. The moment can be read as a parable about the spectator's involvement with comic characters: we think we're humouring them, but they may be indulging *us*, taking note of the blind spots and double-dealings which inform our own eccentricities. Hardcastle's point about Marlow is apposite: 'What a fool was I, to think a young man could learn modesty by travelling. He might as soon learn wit at a masquerade.' The joke is not just on Marlow's or on Hardcastle's folly. This is a gibe and a wink at the maskers in the audience—and at any others who flatter themselves that their own characters are immune to role play.

So far, then, our understanding of comic character could be heard as a response to the Socratic imperative, 'Know Thyself.' Comedy, if it were a character, might reply: 'To thine own *selves* be true,' or 'To one's own conflicts be true.' This is one reason why comic writers and artists have often gravitated towards versions of masquerade and carnival. In *Don Juan* (1819–24), Byron referred to 'the truth in masquerade', and his adventures at Italian carnivals led him to suggest that, in the midst of them, 'Life becomes for a moment a drama without the fiction.' What, Byron seems to be asking, might come from taking yourself as a kind of joke? Can a comic approach to character provide insight via illusion? At some 18th-century masquerades, participants did not just impersonate anybody, but the opposite of what they took themselves to be (servants came as royalty; pimps as cardinals; ladies as gentlemen), or they came in two-in-one disguises, combining opposites in a single costume. The implication is that we are always other than what we really want to be, or that we are most alive when indulging in a fantasy of ourselves. As Oscar Wilde put it: 'One's real life is so often the life that one does not lead.' The comedy of the carnivalesque is privy to this secret, as Byron acknowledged in *Beppo* (1818):

> The moment night with dusky mantle covers
> The skies (and the more duskily the better),
> The time less liked by husbands than by lovers
> Begins, and prudery flings aside her fetter;
> And gaiety on restless tiptoe hovers,
> Giggling with all the gallants who beset her;

And there are songs and quavers, roaring, humming,
Guitars, and every other sort of strumming.

The stanza dances by in a beguiling whirl—so quickly, in fact, that
there's little time to register the small print hidden in 'prudery
flings aside her fetter'. If Prudery herself does this, then she isn't
really a prude—or, at least, not irretrievably so. The personification
is Byron's way of saying that the single-minded person is itself a
kind of fiction. As the poet confessed in *Don Juan*: 'I almost think
the same skin, | For one without, has two or three within.'

## Playing up

Byron is part of a long, illustrious family of writers who have
grasped that comedy is often the most effective way of blowing the
gaff on myths that cluster around the idea of character. In the
Victorian period character was increasingly seen as an evaluative as
well as a descriptive term, a calling card for a lady or gentleman 'of
character'. The devastatingly debonair achievements of W. S. Gilbert, Oscar Wilde, and Noël Coward glide in and out of this
territory. In Gilbert's *Engaged* (1877), the charade that sometimes
passes for romantic courtship is exposed for what it is. Belvawney is
happy to marry whichever of two ladies that Cheviot doesn't:
'Ladies, one word before I go,' he coos. 'I love you, whichever you
are, with a fervour which I cannot describe in words…I will devote
my life to proving that I love you and you only, whichever it may be.'
Cheviot himself goes one better: 'Symperson, I never loved three
girls as I loved those three—never! never!' This is a twist on the old
routine in which characters were stereotypes. Now, instead, they
treat others as expendable types, because the marriage market is a
money market. Parodies of sentiment are now the real thing, part of
the artifice of everyday life. Modern people, the drama patiently
explains, really are like this.

The actors of farce should play the absurdity of their characters
with a straight face—after all, this is what some members of their

audience do outside the theatre. Besides, people do not always see other people for who they are, but see substitutions for them, people they want or would prefer them to be. So when, in *The Importance of Being Earnest* (1895), Cecily falls for Algernon before meeting him she is not doing anything so very unusual. He laments that he hasn't even written her love letters. Not a problem, she points out: 'I was forced to write your letters for you. I wrote always three times a week, and sometimes oftener.' This is absurd yet also absurdly true; we can and do fall into the scripts that others' fantasies have written for us. When Algernon asks her a moment later what would happen if his name wasn't Ernest, Cecily replies: 'I might respect you, Ernest, I might admire your character, but I fear that I should not give you my undivided attention.' It's not entirely clear whether 'you' and 'your character' are split or allied, but what is clear is that neither is enough to secure a winning combination. Such agile pirouetting carries a serious point, which might be translated into Wildean form:

READER: 'A play about two men whose lovers insist that they change their names before they can be married? How farcical!'
AUTHOR: 'Really? Women have to do it every day.'

Comic character finds a welcome home in farce because farce can make delusion seem ludic. Melodrama is played as camp; people don't exactly labour under misapprehensions, but juggle with them. In Noël Coward's *Hay Fever* (1925), the Bliss family—which includes an actress, a caricaturist, and a novelist—is intent on letting life take its lead from art. 'I feel most colossally temperamental—I should like to kiss you and kiss you and kiss you and break everything in the house and then jump into the river,' Simon says to Myra, as though making a scene was one of the most worthwhile things you could do with your time. On occasion, a comic approach to life gives you permission to play at not quite being yourself whilst you also see through such playing. And yet, within this, the feeling lingers that you could *become* your most theatrical self by the time comedy is through with you. 'Let's have that nice little intrigue,' David whispers to Myra. 'I love to see

45

things as they are first, and then pretend they're what they're not.' Affectation is the route to a revitalized sense of individuality. By keeping up their acts, the Blisses blithely roll a wrecking ball through the tired English need to keep up appearances. In *Hay Fever*, as so often in comedy, true character finds a way of turning airs and graces into a liberating kind of grace.

'I hate to seem inquisitive, but would you kindly inform me who I am?' Jack asks in *The Importance of Being Earnest*. From Menander to Wilde and beyond, this question is *the* comic question. It implies that—in this universe at least—character is social, something you frequently have to enquire after through repartee and exchange. In comedy, it seems that only other people know who we are, or are in a position to know who we are. Maybe that's why some analysts, when confronted by comedy, feel the urge to make the most sweeping of identifications. 'One critic asserted that I was the symbolic embodiment of all persecuted Jews for 2,000 years,' observed Groucho Marx. 'What sort of goddamned review is that?' Who wants to be a symbol? Yet the idea of comedy as the reaching and searching for character is close to the zany heart of Marxian patter. As in the *commedia dell'arte*, the brothers' act often shuttles back and forth between the predictable and the spontaneous, between a stock, static persona on the one hand and a creative ad-lib on the other (overseeing the brothers' rehearsals, their co-writer George Kaufman once noted, 'I may be wrong, but I think I just heard one of the original lines'). Groucho continually stepped in and out of character when performing, which is fitting because the mercurial nature of character is what so many of the films are about. In *Animal Crackers* (1930), for example:

GROUCHO: Say, I used to know a fellow that looked exactly like you by the name of Emanuel Ravelli. Are you his brother?
CHICO: I'm Emanuel Ravelli.
GROUCHO: Well, no wonder you look like him. But I still insist there is a resemblance.

Doubles are everywhere, from the miracle of the mirror scene in *Duck Soup* (1933)—where Chico and Groucho find a wonderful visual language to show that one can indeed resemble one's brother and oneself at the same time—to *A Night at the Opera* (1935), where Groucho attempts to soothe a jealous Mrs Claypool: 'That woman? Do you know why I sat with her? Because she reminded me of you...That's why I'm sitting here with you, because you remind me of you. Your eyes, your throat, your lips, everything about you reminds me of you, except you.' The joyful desperation here portends both anarchy and ease. There's nobody, it seems, that we resemble less than ourselves, yet we are never more ourselves than when we are reminded of the fact.

If the key outline of comic character could be sketched in one image, perhaps this is what it might look like (see Figure 7).

'It's Our *Own* Story *Exactly*! He Bold as a Hawk, She Soft as the Dawn'

7. James Thurber, cartoon in *The New Yorker* (25 February 1939)

This is another sprightly take on the way people are drawn to imagining themselves as part of a double act in order to shore up their own sense of identity. We laugh here at the wife for her endearing misunderstanding of herself and her other half, but this is also Our *Own* Story *Exactly*. We are laughing, too, at the odd, enduring romance of our need to look for types, our need to find ourselves in types and to *be* types, even as we continue to seek new ways of finding our opposites attractive. Baudelaire once claimed that, to nurture a sense of the comic, a person should foster 'the capacity of being himself and someone else at the same time'. This might explain why it so often seems that, when enjoying comic characters, we are spectating and participating at the same time, as if the joke is on both them and us. Towards the end of Howard Hawks's film *Bringing Up Baby* (1938), one incredulous character yells: 'They're all impersonating somebody!' Aren't we all?

# Chapter 4
# Plotting mischief

GWENDOLEN: The suspense is terrible. I hope it will last.

Oscar Wilde, *The Importance of Being Earnest* (1895)

## Punchlines and plotlines

Comedy holds out for good times through the art of good timing. Some jokes even make wasting time feel like an activity you'd want to be involved in—Richard Pryor once began a set with: 'I'd like to make you laugh for about ten minutes. Though I'm gonna be on for an hour.' A joke is often a scaled-down story, so it's a useful place to start when thinking about how comic forms conceive and practise the art of storytelling. Cicero observed that 'the most common kind of joke is that in which we expect one thing and another is said; here our own disappointed expectation makes us laugh'. Immanuel Kant followed this up by stressing the temporal aspect of comic experience: '*Laughter is an affect resulting from the sudden transformation of a heightened expectation into nothing.*' This is suggestive, although perhaps '*nothing*' under-describes what happens to expectations when they are not quite met. Playing for laughs involves playing for and with time, and it nurtures a certain kind of rhythm.

Comedy has frequently been the art of springing surprises, but established routine is what makes surprise possible (see Figure 8).

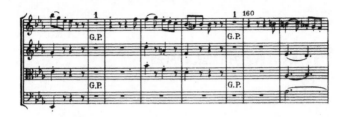

8. Joseph Haydn, String Quartet in E flat Major, Opus 33, No. 2, 'The Joke' (1781)

The ending of Haydn's quartet (aptly nicknamed 'The Joke') has three general pauses to encourage a sense that the parallel phrases will continue, and also to accentuate a feeling of completion at the end of the fourth phrasing. This 'closure', followed by the longest pause of all, implies that the piece is over only for the music to start up again with a repetition of the opening phrase, which itself then becomes the final cadence. My mirthless description of the thing is as brief as I could make it, but when you actually hear Haydn's piece it's hard not to smile—as the musicians playing it usually do. If 'The Joke' were a sentence, it would read as if all the full stops were suddenly changed to commas, and vice versa. So maybe a semi-colon is an apt marker for the kind of pause that comedians are frequently after, one which invites appreciation of the laughable surprise not so much as a response to the shift from something into '*nothing*', but as signal that we have learnt to read something in more than one way. The writer A. P. Herbert artfully hinted as much when thinking over the secret of comic timing: 'The essence of humour is surprise; that is why you laugh when you see a joke in *Punch*.'

Some evolutionary theories of how jokes work also focus on temporal considerations. According to Matthew Hurley, Daniel Dennett, and Reg Adams, the success story of human evolution is based on 'anticipation-generation', on jumping to conclusions as deftly and as swiftly as possible. We have become virtuoso expecters of things, and jokes draw attention to our reliance on patterns of inference. So, they argue, jokes came into being as a way for us to check and to maintain 'data integrity': the surprise that is the essence of humour is really 'the detection of a false belief in a mental space'. Our laughter when we get a joke announces a triumph: the salvaging of cognitive prowess from momentary weakness. In other words, jokes ensure our quick-wittedness is kept quick. In a safe testing ground, we suddenly understand and correct the error of our ways.

This theory explains much, although some jokes are visions of a less straightforwardly utilitarian life. They offer not just a training in timeliness, but also a counter-intuitive celebration of the false beliefs themselves. Take Woody Allen's recourse to his own timekeeper: 'I'm proud of this pocket watch. My grandfather, on his deathbed, sold me this watch.' It's a good Jewish joke, and more. Although plotted so as to provide a gentle rebuke to the audience's and to Woody's great expectations, it also shares and delights in the grandfather's refusal to bow to the pressures of circumstance. Time is the one thing we cannot control, yet the immaculate timing of the best jokes implies that we can. Their very neatness is a riposte to—and consolation for—the messiness of mortality. This isn't only a lesson in the value of adaptive behaviour. After all, Grandpa no longer has any need to plan ahead, but he's going to plan anyway. The economy of the one-liner may acknowledge that time is money, but the jest also encourages us to indulge in surreptitious, purposeless plotting just for the hell of it—or simply to see what might come of it.

The contours of joke structures, their dual allegiance to ordered shapeliness and to shock tactics, are writ large in comic plots from

*Menander* to *Zoolander*. A tripartite rhythm emerges: set-up; elaboration (which usually involves misunderstandings); resolution. In Donatus's *Fragment on Comedy and Tragedy* (*c.*350) the plot's stages are termed *protasis*, *epitasis*, and *catastrophe*. Unlike tragedy, though, the comic plot is presided over by the fickle goddess *Tyche* (in the Roman scheme *Fortuna*), a forerunner of Lady Luck. August Wilhelm von Schlegel felt that in Roman comedy 'the place of Destiny is supplied by Chance' and Susan Langer claims that 'Tragedy is the image of Fate, as comedy is of Fortune.' Western comedy's fortunes owe much to Terence here. His innovation was to underscore the anything-could-happen-next feeling of comedy by removing the divine prologue. 'Don't expect me to tell you the plot,' quips the actor of the Prologue to *The Brothers* (160 BC). Terence's adaptation of his Greek sources also led to another bequest: the double plot. These plots usually revolve around the wayward love lives of two young couples, so the drama's content shares the form's emphasis on unpredictability. As Parmeno explains to one lovelorn gallant at the beginning of the *The Eunuch* (161 BC): 'if a matter has no plan or control to it at all, you can't manage it according to a plan'. The 'matter' here is amorous desire. For Terence and his many followers, to be in love is to have lost the plot.

But that's just one side of the story. Lovers yearn for consummation, and comedy is frequently in league with serendipity. The narratives that comprise the Terentian double plot mirror each other, and this tends to focus attention on the situation rather than the characters. Even disarray seems mathematically structured as the audience is encouraged to detect safety in numbers and patterns. Despite the entanglements of circumstance, comedy's heroes and heroines gravitate towards one another via coincidences that seem more than merely coincidental. 'Citizens, is there anyone luckier than me alive today?' Chaerea asks the audience in *The Eunuch*. 'So many good things have so suddenly come together for me!' It's as though fate and fortune are being blended rather than simply opposed.

Chaerea doesn't know whether to thank his own presence of mind or Fortuna, and in *The Brothers* Micio offers clarification: 'the life of man is like a game of dice: if the throw doesn't give you the number you most need, you have to use your skill to make the best of the number it does happen to give you'. Comedy, we could say, has recurrently made the best of things through a master plot that riffs on the mercurial operations of Hap. The story usually begins with the mishap; then, via something haphazard, characters happen upon a happy coincidence; then, through a certain amount of happy skill and happenstance, things happily turn out for the best. To put it this way is to draw attention to the sheer amount of hap that goes into happiness. And yet comic plotting also suggests that happiness consists in taking your chances. As Louis Pasteur observed: 'Chance favours only the prepared mind.'

## Allowing for accidents

Comedy is often a story in which people *can* believe their luck. While predestination is underplayed, prestidigitation is highlighted. Perhaps this is why the creators of comic plots have so regularly called upon the services of the Trickster—the Hermes figure that James Joyce described as 'an accident of providence'. Accidents will happen, and one pleasure of watching comedies lies in seeing how characters and their creators extricate themselves from the tight spots. Niccolò Machiavelli's plot structures are exemplary models here, and they take their bearings from the Roman tradition which emphasized Fortune's favouring of the brave. *The Mandrake* (1518) centres on Callimaco's scheme to get Lucrezia, the wife of Nicia, into bed. The married couple are in need of a son but it appears that Nicia is impotent, so the trickster figure Ligurio is enlisted to devise an intrigue to help Callimaco out. True to type, Ligurio is sure that 'everything will turn out right in the end'. The character's craftiness stands as an emblem of his author's craft, orchestrating events through a careful timing of entrances and exits.

*The Mandrake* echoes Machiavelli's political thinking in *The Prince* (1513) by depicting a world in which the only way to avoid becoming a victim of Fortuna is to keep out-scheming the schemers (the end of the play even contains a hint that Lucrezia herself is not so much a naïve dupe, but rather a willing accomplice). If comedy registers the importance of the operations of Chance, it also prompts reflection on whether Chance might not be a misprint for Choice. In many comic plots, submission to the doubtful activity of chancing it seems to be the main criterion for a character's volition. Small wonder that the restless trickster is so at home in the genre. His yearning for a plot (any plot really, but the trickier the better) signals a relish for agency, an agency that only really knows and feels itself whilst committing to new forms of risk. Ligurio's last appearance in *The Mandrake* clinches the point. His sigh of contentment quickly modulates into a note of expectancy: 'Everything has turned out just as I had predicted. Now what do we do?'

If comedy has a passion for plotting mischief, it should also be acknowledged that comic capital has often been made from plans going awry. Ligurio's 'Now what do we do?' could reasonably be challenged by Oberon's question to Puck in *A Midsummer Night's Dream*: 'What hast thou done? Thou hast mistaken quite.' This leads us to the other, equally pronounced enthusiasm of comic plot makers: their cherishing of incompetence and their fondness for a certain kind of botched job. The shaggy-dog story, the cock-and-bull story, the preposterously prolix story—all are a vital part of the story of comedy. We like to laugh, it seems, at things going wrong. Laurence Sterne delights in this wrongness in *The Life and Opinions of Tristram Shandy, Gentleman* (1759–67). Tristram's attempt to describe his life is itself the biggest joke in the book, for although he understands that a plot should eke out causality (A led to B which allowed C), he's also troubled by the fact that Z owes a fair bit to Y, and that you can't really appreciate Y until you understand X. Tristram doesn't even manage to narrate his birth until nearly halfway through the novel, so caught up is he by the earlier tale of his begetting, and by the contributing causes to that event, and so on and so forth. Sterne is drawing on a heritage which has conceived the comic as a *diversion* in the full sense of that word. Detour takes precedence over destination. Paul Klee once observed that 'drawing is taking a line for a walk'. Just over 300 pages into his novel, Tristram gives a drawing of his life story which suggests rather that he has been taken for a walk by the line (see Figure 9).

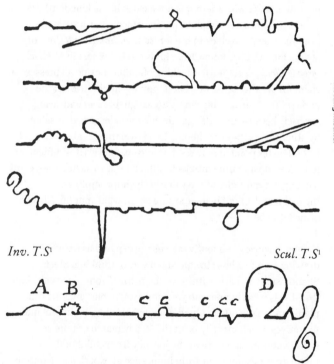

*Inv. T.S*[1]

*Scul. T.S*[1]

9. Sterne, *Tristram Shandy*, vol. VI, chapter XL

Squiggles and letters mark digressions and other infelicitous moments where chronology was waylaid. What we have here is the comedy of errors, an image of a person who is not quite conducting his life, but chasing it down.

Sterne's novel envisages itself as part of the great comic family by noting from the start that it has particular trouble with clocks. Tristram's mother's untimely question to his father during sex—'*Pray, my dear, have you not forgot to wind up the clock?*'—is even seen by the hero as the cause of his own problems in sticking to the task in hand, and later he offers a mini-digression in parentheses: '(I wish there was not a clock in the kingdom)'. Clocks organize the progress of plots, but in comedy they are not always present ('there's no clock in the forest' in *As You Like It*), or not always followed (as John Cleese finds out to his cost in Michael Frayn's *Clockwise* (1986)). Clocking off in Sterne's novel presses the claim for another sense of what happiness might involve: the hapless. Tristram and his family are laughable *and* endearing precisely because their designs for life are sidetracked or sabotaged by other things they care about. 'In a novel there is always a clock,' E. M. Forster pointed out. Yes, but in comic novels it is difficult to make out what time the clock will tell next. In such guises, comic plotting is a reminder of the value of the impromptu and the incidental, of not being too sure about what your life story is meant to be.

Comedy's stories frequently take us unprepared as a way of drawing us into a less straitjacketed way of thinking. Sterne's Shandeism is an early witness to the truth of John Lennon's claim that 'life is what happens to you while you're busy making other plans', and many other comedies enjoy resisting developmental narratives which breezily posit the steady march of time as synonymous with progress: the journey from childhood to maturity, for example, or from innocence to experience. Nonsense literature shares this take on things, playing around with progress narratives through appeals to the child in us. Lewis Carroll's *The*

*Hunting of The Snark* (1876) begins with the Bellman telling his crew: 'Just the place for a Snark! I have said it thrice: | What I tell you three times is true.' Three is the magic number. It portends order and orientation, and it's the minimum number required for pattern recognition. But three is also the number of pauses Haydn plotted in 'The Joke' so as to set a trap for expectation, and in many jokes the third part of the triad brings a sudden shift of perceptual horizons. Carroll's poem is primed and timed to become a parody of a quest narrative. Its denouement sees the Baker's final discovery cut short: 'It's a Boo—'. The closing stanza fills in the blank:

In the midst of the word he was trying to say,
In the midst of his laughter and glee,
He had softly and suddenly vanished away—
For the Snark *was* a Boojum, you see.

This leaves readers none the wiser, whilst also gently casting aspersions on the need to *become* wiser—whether through a wild goose chase for the Boojum or through a need to hunt down 'the moral of the story'. Nonsense takes special delight in turning orders of succession into non sequiturs, and it's close to the heart of comic plotting as Carroll and others have practised it.

*Alice's Adventures in Wonderland* (1865) involves a similar kind of snark hunt. When court is in session, the King offers sage counsel on tale-telling—'Begin at the beginning and go on till you come to the end: then stop'—but he's in the wrong genre. After Alice steps through the looking glass, she sprints with the Queen for some minutes only to find herself in the same location: ' "Well, in *our* country," said Alice, still panting a little, "you'd generally get to somewhere else—if you ran very fast for a long time as we've been doing." "A slow sort of country!" said the Queen. "Now, *here*, you see, it takes all the running *you* can do, to keep in the same place." ' This sounds nonsensical, yet many of us know the feeling. Wittgenstein felt that such dilemmas could be catalysts for new ways of living and thinking: 'if the place I want to get to could only be reached by way of a ladder, I would give up trying to get there. For the place I really have to get to is a place I must already be at now.' This reflection is part of a consideration of what could be gained by untethering the idea of progress from that of a narrative or a clear-cut 'move forward'. Fittingly, given his love of comedy and nonsense, the epigraph Wittgenstein chose for his *Philosophical Investigations* (1953) was taken from Johann Nestroy's comedy, *Der Schützling* (1847): 'It is in the nature of progress that it looks much greater than it really is.' Comedians across the ages have shown a wry appreciation of this fact.

## Calling time

So comic plotting may involve a questioning *of* plot, an enquiry into received opinions about causality, development, and sense-making. 'Time wounds all heels,' as one spoonerism has it. The phrase could stand as shorthand for the preposterous action and insight of comedy. Indeed, the claim is perhaps truer than the proverb it revises, for none of us is getting any younger. Yet, true to comic form, somehow the play on words here lessens the blow to one's Achilles heel. Verbal wit makes time's power a little less consequential by making quick work of syntactical sequence, the very marker of time in language. Theatrical comedy has won analogous victories by putting time itself on stage and then plotting ways for humans to try its strength. Take pantomime, for instance; in Thomas Dibdin's *Mother Goose* (1807), we see:

> [CLOWN *and* PANTALOON] *endeavour to secure* HARLEQUIN, *who eludes their grasp, and leaps through the face of the clock, which immediately presents a* SPORTSMAN *with his gun cocked. The* CLOWN *opens the clock door, and a little* HARLEQUIN *appears as the pendulum, the* CLOWN *saying 'Present! Fire!' The* SPORTSMAN *lets off his piece, the* CLOWN *falls down, during which period* COLUMBINE *and* HARLEQUIN, *who had previously entered through the panel, escape. After some tricks, the* CLOWN *runs off in pursuit.*

In 18th- and 19th-century pantomime, clocks arrive in the nick of time. They are utilized to escape the exigencies of the moment, and paradoxically become the vehicles by which time itself is resisted. Here the clock stands as a transformative threshold; it turns people into timepieces as a way of keeping them safe from harm. Later in *Mother Goose* 'Pantaloon *mounts the dial and the* Clown *clings around it—ascending in this situation.*' Clown is the Trickster reincarnated. As his hands seek out a communion with the hands of the clock, we can be sure that time is on his side.

The breakneck speed of Clown and his associates seems to imply that no harm will ever really come to them (recall Ionesco's suggestion that tragedy is comedy speeded up). The Theatre of the Absurd is indebted to pantomime, and to the pace of slapstick (Ionesco once said that the three biggest influences on his work were Groucho, Chico, and Harpo Marx). In this kind of theatre, plots do not so much thicken as quicken. Ionesco's first play, *The Bald Soprano* (1950), opens with a stage direction announcing that '*The English clock strikes 17 English strokes.*' A few minutes later, '*The clock strikes as much as it likes.*' His drama zeroes in on forms of expectation which build up around the domestic interior—the expectation to 'get on' in life, to get married, to have people round for dinner, and associated horrors—but they do so at an odd speed. 'The essence of the comic,' the playwright ventured, is 'a kind of acceleration of movement,' so when Berenger turns to Daisy in *Rhinoceros* (1959) and says, 'Oh dear! In the space of a few minutes we've gone through twenty-five years of married life,' the thing is appalling yet strangely bearable.

In *Amédée, or How to Get Rid of It* (1954), a couple debate what to do with a corpse that is growing in their house. It's a skeleton spilling out of their cupboard, and the eerie comedy is intensified as Ionesco draws attention to the clock onstage: '*The audience should still be able to see its hands, moving slowly at the same speed as the dead man's feet...the body is still imperceptibly lengthening, the hands of the clock are gradually advancing.*' At the end of the play, though, Amédée takes off, utilizing the by-now-gigantic head of the corpse as a balloon (we are again back with 'Clown, *ascending in this situation*'). In *Jack, or The Submission* (1955), Jack's family push him into an arranged marriage, and the plot only gets going once his sister breaks some devastating news: 'I'm going to tell you the whole thing in twenty-seven words. Here it is, and try to remember it: You are chronometrable.' Modern comedy has often been drawn to such accelerated learning curves. Although its depictions of chronometrable lives plotted and then run on fast-forward can be unnerving, the laughter which these depictions frequently inspire can also be a blessed relief. Noël Coward explains: 'You live and learn. Then you die and forget it all.'

But what if you live and learn and *don't* die? This is the predicament and privilege of weatherman Phil Connors in one of the finest cinematic comedies of modern times, one that weaves together many of the issues raised in this chapter: *Groundhog Day* (1993). Phil (played by Bill Murray) wakes up to find that he's repeating the same day over and over, stuck in a time loop (even suicide isn't an option; like another version of Clown, who falls down only to bounce back up, each time Phil kills himself he wakes up again at 6 a.m. on Groundhog Day, 2nd February). Replaying variations of the same joke over and over, *Groundhog Day* is the *reductio ad absurdum* of the comic plot, although the absurdity becomes the vehicle for the film's uncanny realism. In the bar Phil turns desperately to the man next to him and asks, 'What would *you* do if you were stuck in one place, and every day was exactly the same, and nothing that you did mattered?' The man replies: 'That about sums it up for me.'

And yet, as so often with comic forms, the timekeepers in the background offer us not so much a summing-up, as a multiplication of possibility. In the café, in between huge mouthfuls of coffee and cake, Phil explains the situation to his colleague Rita (see Figure 10).

**10.** *Groundhog Day* (1993)

At first glance, it looks like two of the three stopped clocks on the wall behind him are telling the same time, but on closer inspection it's clear that one reads five minutes to six, and the other half-past eleven. So apparent repetition discloses a difference. Perhaps the timings whisper a hope about life lived *as* a comedy: there can be room for manoeuvre in even the most deterministic of environments. The date, too, may contain a similar hope, for February ushers in carnival time across the globe, a time that resists the onward pressure of quotidian clocking. Groundhog Day is the time of comedy: it may feel initially like Fate, but the second day of the second month is really a day for second chances.

The film combines two prominent traditions and tropes of comic story-making—let's call them 'Machiavellian meticulousness' and 'Shandean straying'. First Phil takes up the mantle of Trickster and seeks to convert the alarming excess of déjà vu into an opportunity: there are to be no repercussions (time is to be reset at the end of each day anyway), so he starts to scheme by plotting thefts, bouts of bed-hopping and other crimes and misdemeanours. However, as time does and doesn't go on, it dawns on him that if he has nothing to lose, he has nothing to gain, nothing to keep hold of. A life lacking in consequence, it turns out, is not really something you can commit to. Little by little, Phil stops thinking of his life as a plot or as an occasion for plotting (trying to get Rita into bed, for example), and opts for a more digressive, less instrumental approach. He reads poetry, takes up the piano, helps out around town, not with ulterior motives exactly, but more with a need to be involved in the activities themselves, lead where they may.

The song that Phil and all audiences of the film grow sick of (it's playing every morning at six on the radio) is Sonny and Cher's 'I Got You Babe'. The scriptwriter Danny Rubin has drawn attention to the fact that the song has a false ending (it plays a similar trick to Haydn's joke quartet), so it's a fitting soundtrack for Phil's situation. But it also contains a line that answers back to those who think only of the future: 'at least I'm sure of all the things we got'. *Groundhog Day* becomes a testament to the value of living in the moment without being wholly captive to it. 'I'm happy *now*,' Phil says, simultaneously falling in love with Rita and falling out of the time loop. Like many of the best jokes and comedies, the film seems to warn against our developing too clear a sense of what the future will or should be. Indeed, many versions of comic plotting intimate not only that there's no time like the present, but also that there's no time *but* the present. In a deleted line from an early version of the screenplay, Phil finally wakes up to a new life by realizing that 'if you use time wisely, there's never enough of it'. This hints at the attraction of comedy itself. The form's own wise use of time and timing is one reason why we continue to need it.

# Chapter 5
# **Underdogs**

I do not know that I have a carefully thought-out theory on
exactly what makes people laugh, but the premise of all
comedy is a man in trouble, the little guy against the big guy.

Jerry Lewis

## In thrall to folly

Why go and see a comedy? In Plato's *Republic* (380 BC), Socrates
suggests that we enjoy the spectacle of others doing the ridiculous
things we'd secretly like to do ourselves. 'You were afraid of being
thought a buffoon,' he explains, so you went to watch buffoonery
instead. However, 'having stimulated the risible faculty at the
theatre, you are betrayed unconsciously to yourself into playing
the comic poet at home'. Perhaps, although there are worse parts
to play. Socrates's argument may itself be shadowed by irony (he
could be playing devil's advocate as a way of encouraging further
reflection) and he certainly cuts an enigmatic figure elsewhere in
Plato, acting stupid or gently laughing to himself as he hazards an
opinion. He blends the attributes of two archetypal comic
characters—the Buffoon (*bomolochus*) and the Ironical type
(*eiron*)—knowingly playing dumb as a way of playing around with
the limits of knowledge. Comedy often takes this ludic approach
to wisdom by calling upon the services of a particular set of

characters. When, in *The Gay Science* (1882), Friedrich Nietzsche turns his attentions to 'the delight in simulation, the inner craving for a role and mask', he names the key suspects: 'the actor, the "artist" (the zany, the teller of lies, the buffoon, fool, clown at first, as well as the classical servant)'. Quite a roll call. This chapter explores how the members of this motley crew are related, and what they might be up to.

Nietzsche suggests that the comedian's inner craving is most often observable in 'the lower classes', and from the beginning comic instincts have been in league with various kinds of lowness. In the *Poetics* (*c.*335 BC), Aristotle says that comedy is 'an imitation of characters of a lower type' (often with a demotic style to match), and the Roman grammarian Donatus suggests that the mode is 'low-footed': 'it does not contain the business of those living in towers and upper floors but those living in a low and humble place'. The comedy of Plautus keeps its ear close to this ground. The dramatist was himself low-footed; his name is a variant form of *planipes* ('flatfoot'), used as a nickname for barefoot Latin mimes in which he may have appeared. He brought one particular vagabond centre stage: the *servus callidus*, or clever slave. This tricky customer is often a surrogate for the artist himself. When plotting his deceptions, for instance, Pseudolus thinks of the writer: 'he makes a fiction look very much like a fact. That's what I'll do; I'll be a poet.'

The slave's frequent addresses to the audience also imply that he's one of us. He stands at the threshold between stage and world, prompting consideration of how his fictional antics are a part of life—and part of the way in which we make fictions out of our lives. Most often, he reminds us that we are laughable creatures. 'We're all fools though we don't know it,' says Pseudolus, 'for running so hard after this or that, as if we could possibly tell for ourselves what's good for us and what isn't...But enough of this philosophizing. I do run on, don't I?' He's another version of the *eiron* who might or might not be playing the fool. No wonder Simo warns Callipho to be careful: 'he'll talk your head off till you feel as if you're arguing with Socrates instead of Pseudolus'. So the down-at-heel trickster is a spur to serious thinking. In the first scene, Pseudolus warns members of the audience 'to be on their guard…against me…and not to trust a word I say'. This spin on the Cretan paradox captures the essence of the figure and our relations with him. If we're his confidants, then we may also be his dupes. If we're with him, then he might be against us. As Tranio points out to the audience in *The Haunted House*: 'safety's unsafe, too'.

The slave's dizzying attraction to joking, paradox, and irony in Roman comedy makes him difficult to read. He is often called upon to solve a problem he himself has created, so he is saviour as well as scapegoat—a man who must kowtow to the established powers even as he finds (or stumbles upon) loopholes in the law. This scoundrel has many afterlives in comedy, not least in the *commedia dell'arte*, where the evolution of the stock character of the Zany witnesses a split into two figures: the dim-witted, country bumpkin and the cunning, creative servant. The related figure of the fool, both idiot and iconoclast, develops along similarly mixed bloodlines. 'Fool' (from the Latin *follem, follis,* meaning 'bellows') was originally employed in the sense of 'windbag', 'empty-headed person' (*OED*), but the figure can also usher in winds of change, helping to stoke fires that the authorities may find hard to put out. Actor and writer Dario Fo has noted of fools, clowns, and their ilk that 'the problem they invariably pose is—who's in command, who's the boss?' They pose this problem by inviting consideration of the very nature of the pose itself. If they cannot be taken at face value, then who can? Is any act of 'command' itself a kind of pose? What does the boss have to hide in order to *be* the boss?

In secular as well as religious varieties, the discourse of Folly encourages this spirit of enquiry, and its interest in doubleness and double-dealing becomes a formative influence on comedy from the Renaissance onwards. What languages of folly and comedy often share is the suspicion that mankind's high-mindedness might be a bit of a joke. Desiderius Erasmus is a key figure here. As the title suggests, his *The Praise of Folly* (1511) is shaped as a paradoxical encomium and a critique of 'wisemen and deep philosophers' (the first English translation refers to this tribe as '*foolosophers*'). Praise is reserved instead for the foolishly wise (the *morosophos*), those underdogs who have often been dismissed as 'dolts, simpletons, nincompoops'. Erasmus's speaker, Folly herself, notes that 'Fools provide the very thing for which princes are always on the lookout: jokes, laughs, guffaws, fun. And don't forget another talent, by no means contemptible, that is peculiar to fools: they alone speak the plain, unvarnished truth.' This journey—from contemptible outcast to court jester to valued truth teller—has an analogue in the voyage of the holy fool.

Christ is an exemplary case (the man who hangs out with dropouts, talks a strange kind of parabolic nonsense, and rides to victory on a donkey). Folly explains: 'Christ, though he was the wisdom of the Father, became somehow foolish in order to relieve the folly of mortals when he took on human nature and appeared in the form of a man.' This develops St Paul's emphasis on the sanctity of true folly. Like the incongruity at the heart of the Incarnation, foolishness disrupts any tidy sense of hierarchy. It betokens a certain kind of folly, then, to shun the insights of the fool: 'If any man among you seemeth to be wise in this world, let him become a fool, that he may be wise. For the wisdom of this world is foolishness with God' (*1 Corinthians* iii. 18–19). So the fool is a low life but also a warning to those who are solely intent on living the high life. He judges those who judge him. The figure reflects back—and reflects upon—the realities we try to evade. No wonder he inspires such mixed feelings.

## Awkward questions

The fool has proved to be an enduring bequest to comic forms. Shakespeare's plays often circle round distinctions between the

'natural' fool (a person 'congenitally deficient in reasoning powers')
and the 'artificial' fool ('a professional fool or jester'—*OED*),
teasing the audience to consider when and why the distinctions
don't hold up. In *All's Well That Ends Well* (*c.*1604–5), the braggart
Parolles turns to Lavatch the Clown: 'Go to, thou art a witty fool; I
have found thee.' Lavatch's reply cuts to the heart of the matter:
'Did you find me in your self, sir? Or were you taught to find me?'
A hit, a very palpable hit, although 'fool' is rarely just a term of
abuse in Shakespeare. Rather, a state of foolishness is something to
aspire to. In *As You Like It*, Jacques sighs: 'O, that I were a fool! |
I am ambitious for a motley coat.' Folly is disguised acuity, as
the Duke appreciates when summing up the man in motley: 'He
uses his folly like a stalking-horse and under the presentation of
that he shoots his wit.'

So it appears that there are two types of fool—the unwitting and
the more knowing variety—but what the second type knows and
seeks to make known is that nobody is fully in control of who they
are. Wit is a weapon of distinction, yet those who wield it best
sense that they are nothing special. When, in *Twelfth Night*
(*c.*1601–2), Viola says of Feste that 'he's wise enough to play the
fool, | And to do that well craves a kind of wit', she pays him this
compliment in response to his own pearl of wisdom: 'Foolery, sir,
does walk about the orb like the sun, it shines everywhere.' Note
'sir' (and recall 'Did you find me in your self, sir?'). Like many
clowns and jesters, Feste minds his manners even as he looks
around him and marks a confederacy of dunces. In Shakespeare
and those who follow his lead, the figure's accent often seeks to
marry supplication and provocation. The coalescence of tones
is apt, because one of comedy's most frequent and enduring
topics is the vexed, intimate relationship between the rulers and
the ruled.

In *Henry IV, Parts I and II* (*c.*1596–8), Falstaff rolls into view as a
blend of heedless clown and wily underling. He is a combination
of buffoon and *eiron*, the great exponent and unmasker of cant.

Prince Hal rightly calls him a 'fool', but he does so without understanding how far the word reaches. Falstaff explains:

> Men of all sorts take pride to gird at me. The brain of this foolish-compounded clay, man, is not able to invent anything that tends to laughter, more than I invent or is invented on me. I am not only witty in myself, but the cause that wit is in other men.

Falstaff is, as Hamlet would say of Elsinore's professional fool, 'a fellow of infinite jest'. Those moments when either the audience or the characters are tempted to feel superior to him are always shadowed by a sense that they've missed the joke and the value of the man—his willingness to draw out the limitations as well as the glories of 'pride', his ability to see through even as he sustains illusion. Hal's ascension to the throne and his casting off of Falstaff ('I know thee not, old man... How ill white hairs become a fool and jester') are couched as a renunciation of comedy, but in Shakespeare the outlook of the fool and jester gives a valuable sense of proportion for superiors if they would but listen. Lear's fool says to his master that 'I had rather be any kind o'thing than a fool. And yet I would not be thee.' In fact, Lear only comes to an enlarged sense of himself as he acknowledges that he too is a 'natural fool', turning to his daughter to admit that 'I am old and foolish.' As so often in the play, the King's fool is one step ahead, for he told the audience much earlier that 'This cold night will turn us all to fools.' Although this cold night seems a long way from comedy, Lear's man is in fact singing an old comic lesson in a tragic key. Puck puts it clearly in *A Midsummer Night's Dream*: 'Lord, what fools these mortals be!'

Erasmus and Shakespeare helped to turn fools and their associates from peripheral dogsbodies into central comic figures. The critic Enid Welsford claimed that 'the Fool is a great untrusser of our slaveries, and comedy is the expression of the spirit of the Fool'. To her credit, though, she immediately added: 'But is that last remark really defensible?' Although the fool is often a defender of freedom, comedy rarely envisages him as completely emancipated. He seems up for revolt, but incapable of revolution. When Freud theorized jokes as phenomena that disavow yet also indulge our rebellious streak ('Only joking,' we say, yet we make the joke nonetheless), he thought of the fool and jester: 'the joke is essentially a double-dealing rogue who serves two masters at once'. We might think of Truffaldino in Carlo Goldoni's *Servant of Two Masters* (1743), hovering between the subservient and the seditious. 'Who the devil are you?' Pantaloon asks Truffaldino. The answer is as riddling as it is clear-cut: 'My master's servant.' This may imply that the rogue is forever locked in, beholden to his role, defined by deference. But the answer's evasiveness also spells trouble, hints at inner resources, invites us to wonder what he's got up his sleeve.

The rise of the modern comic rogue (often a blend of fool and trickster) is marked by a growing sense that the figure contains multitudes, and that this interiority may portend social and political unrest. Because he is so frequently given to employing or exploiting humour as a tool or weapon, he raises the question: what can comedy be used to do? The plays of Pierre Beaumarchais offer some answers. In *The Marriage of Figaro* (1784) the Count tells the servant that 'Your reputation is appalling.' Figaro speaks for himself and for other underdogs when he shoots back: 'Maybe I'm better than my reputation. Do you know many noble lords who could say that?' Beaumarchais was supported and pilloried as critic and ally of the noble lords in the *ancien regime*. In many ways, Figaro is—and was taken to be—his author's slippery surrogate, and if, as Danton argued, 'Figaro killed off the nobility', then he managed the feat by utilizing as well as mocking subservience. In *The Barber of Seville* (1775), in response to Bartholo's claim that 'when I get into an argument with an overbearing ninny, I never back down', Figaro archly replies: 'That's where we differ. I always give in.' *Touché*.

Whatever Beaumarchais's figure has got, it's catching. Just as in Shakespeare, the leading ladies (usually the only characters who can give fools and tricksters a proper run for their money) echo Figaro's endeavours; as the Countess says, 'He exudes such confidence that some of it is wearing off on me.' What this confidence leads to is a sense that the predicament of women is analogous to that of the servant or the dupe. Rosine, Marceline, and others repeatedly ask a central question: 'Is it a crime to want to stop being a slave?' It's not difficult to see why Louis XVI banned the play after one reading; Figaro is not only provocative in himself, but the spur to provocation in others. When he assures his wife, who will later out-trick even him, that 'I'm telling you the most honest truth I know,' she replies: 'You mean there's more than one kind?' This has the hallmarks of a fool's question— apparently perplexed, tacitly acute—and it announces that, though the licensed court fool may have died a death in the 17th century, there were others ready to take up his mantle.

## Clowning around

In his libretto for Mozart's *The Marriage of Figaro* (1786), Lorenzo Da Ponte makes one especially deft addition to Beaumarchais's play. It comes as Figaro watches the Count reading a note which, the valet mistakenly thinks, proves his own wife's infidelity to him: 'I watched him read her note, I watched him laugh, and without realizing it I even laughed at myself.' The complexity of the moment—Figaro pained by laughter yet laughing to relieve his own pain—brings into view a recurring trope in modern comedy. Joe Grimaldi's groundbreaking performance in the role of the pantomime clown is another early version of it; a contemporary reviewer noted that Joe's eyes worked 'without the aid of each other...one eye was quietly silent and serious, whilst the other would be engaged in the most elaborate and mischievous wink'. A captivating mixture of daring, suffering, and impudence, Joe's tag line—'I make you laugh at night but am Grim-All-Day'—signals the reincarnation of a culture hero: the sad clown, a figure who doesn't just act out our unconscious desires, but who also seems tormented by them.

From the 18th century onwards, comedy increasingly imagines the stock type from within, pondering what it would feel like to *be* a fool or clown (see Figure 11).

11. Henry Fuseli, *Fool in a Fool's Cap Having His Portrait Painted* (1757–9)

12. **Nadar and Adrien Tournachon,** *Pierrot the Photographer* (1854–5)

Fuseli's painter is more sprightly than we might expect, his fool less so. It's as though each man holds the key to the other. Similarly, when Felix Tournachon (Nadar) and his brother Adrien photographed the renowned French pantomimist Charles Deburau in his role as Pierrot, they too accentuated the self-reflexive nature of modern clowning (see Figure 12).

What photography and mime share is muteness, yet—as with Chaplin and Keaton later down the line—the silence speaks volumes. Not only does the clown again emerge as the artist's alter ego, he also duplicates the act of spectatorship and suggests that he is taking pictures of us. Fernando Pessoa defined humour as 'the consciousness that what is laughable is akin to ourselves'. This brilliantly captures the humour of such images, and of the clown's significance across the ages in circus and in pantomime. The psychoanalyst Sandor Ferenczi went one step further to claim that one can only ever really laugh at oneself: 'The essence of laughing: How should I like to be as imperfect as that! The essence of laughing at: How satisfactory it is that I am so well behaved, not so imperfect as that!...Behind every laughing at there is concealed unconscious laughing.' So maybe it could be said that we envy the objects of our laughter, and that we need them to remind us of other ways of living. Perhaps this is why the clown figure is so often encountered as part of a pair: White Clown (figure of authority and lucidity, the straight man) and Auguste Clown (the child, the rebel, the upstart); or, in another tradition, Harlequin and Pierrot. Despite their differences, they seem complicit (being funny is not the opposite of being serious, and vice versa). Fellini's films are often haunted by a similar feeling for connection amid opposition, and his love of circus clowns is never very far away from this feeling, as Fellini himself pointed out: 'The game is so real that, if a White Clown is in front of you, you tend to be the Augusto, and vice-versa...the two characters embody a myth that's inside all of us: the reconciliation of opposites.'

The comic partnership we watch is an emblem of the double act we are. Stephen Sondheim's rewrite of Plautus, *A Funny Thing Happened On The Way To The Forum* (1962), makes the scheming Pseudolus play a double role as clown *and* trickster, and reminds us of the figures' shared roots in lowliness: 'comedy tonight', demands Pseudolus, 'Nothing with kings, | Nothing with crowns, | Bring on the lovers, liars and clowns.' We bring them on by looking within: in *A Little Light Music* (1973), Desirée's call to 'send in the clowns' is a euphemism, as Sondheim explained in a later interview: 'the song could have been called "Send in the Fools". I was writing a song in which

Desirée is saying, "aren't we foolish?" or "aren't we fools?"' The ruefully comic rhythm is the one already encountered in many guises and disguises from Plato to Fellini. Folly is the moment in which They becomes We becomes I. To send for the clowns is to send up yourself. When Saul Bellow's character Moses Herzog acknowledges to himself that he is identified by others as '*Thou fool!*' he also secretly knows that '*Not* to be a fool might not be worth the difficult alternatives. Anyway, who was that non-fool?'

If modern fooling is often felt as a deeply private comic sense of self, contemporary culture has also looked for ways to stage this knowledge, to make it into a public event. The fool's latest incarnation is the stand-up comedian, the figure who may at once threaten and forge community, the outsider with inside knowledge. Stand-ups often keep us on our toes by making it hard to pigeonhole them. Like many made-up clowns, Eddie Izzard is—if not exactly genderless—somehow not precisely gendered (he would have his passport read: 'a straight transvestite or a male lesbian'). Comedians can set an example by refusing to follow ours, or by asking where it leads. George Carlin opened his set for *Occupation: Foole* (1973) by admitting that he felt nervous, before quickly turning on the auditorium with: 'You get nervous too, don't you? Audiences have nerves. You get a little nervous, because you know you represent your row, right?' The stand-up is not there to preach to the converted, but to draw attention to what makes them nervous—and to get them to think about it. Faced by a heckler who shouted, 'We don't come to comedy to think!' it is to Bill Hicks's credit that he managed to stay conversable and committed: 'Gee! Where do you go to think? I'll meet you there.'

The best comedians strive to meet the audience halfway, provided that 'the right way' is continually up for debate. As Simon Munnery advises his fellow professionals: 'If the crowd gets behind you, you are facing the wrong way.' Stewart Lee's fascination with the pueblo clowns of South Western America is founded on a similar vision of comedy as a vehicle for discovery via disorientation, and he has argued that modern stand-ups should see themselves as part of a long heritage of 'holy fools, shaman clowns, outsiders'. Lee experienced the pueblo clowns not just as funny, but as frightening, and he notes that this odd combination makes audiences very wary of applauding them. In his own act Lee frequently draws attention to applause as a way of pointing out that clowning around is not just a way of pandering to the crowd. 'I love the sound of one person clapping,' he says. Perhaps because in these moments the joker has managed to bring out a rare truth by dividing opinion in the room. And if applause comes too easy, the comedian has slipped from *agent provocateur* to mere mouthpiece: 'Ah. That's never had a clap before, which probably means it is time to stop doing this show.'

One of the most dazzling recent portraits of the fool combines many of the masks that Nietzsche itemized in *The Gay Science*. He is the archetypal man in trouble, the man who so desperately wants to live life *as* stand-up comedy that he becomes a kind of failed clown: David Brent in *The Office*. David Baddiel suggests that 'what *The Office* is about is comedy; it's about a bloke who thinks he's the funniest person in the room'. Indeed, *The Office* is about why somebody (anybody) would ever *want* to be funny. It reminds us of the always exposed and potentially humiliating position of the stand-up—as though the figure were revisiting, with a view to mastery, the scene of a trauma. Brent plays the joker because he has a fear of being ridiculed. He's trying to forestall the possibility of being laughed at by provoking laughter first ('Always start with a joke,' he explains). How would he describe himself? 'A Friend first, Boss second...probably Entertainer third.' Like many court jesters before him, he is in an ambiguous position of power: he dubs himself The Brentmeister General, yet he's beholden to Head Office—overdog and underdog. In the second series, he thinks of himself as the *callidus servus*, under the thumb of his new boss Neil, but kicking against 'The Powers that Be' and their 'Rule Book'.

He's also the zany who moves funny (think of *that* dance—'I've sort of fused Flashdance with MC Hammer shit'). And, finally, he's the sad clown, given his redundancy notice on Red Nose Day: 'If I make people laugh while I'm saving lives, sue me...I've been made redundant...and now I've got to go and give laughter.'

What Ricky Gervais and Stephen Merchant tap into in *The Office* are the roots of our desire to see foolery in action. If we laugh at David Brent, we laugh partly, uncomfortably, at an exaggeration of our own need to be noticed and to be liked, at our need to hold people's attention and to see ourselves as being able to do this. Which returns us to Socrates's point in the *Republic* about the vicarious pleasure to be had in buffoonery, the way it can offer a strange consolation by externalizing desires and vulnerabilities. Discussing the character of Tim (the witty, unhappy sales rep), Gervais recently commented: 'Tim is us. He's the sort of dissatisfied Socrates in a room of satisfied fools.' This rings true. When Tim says to Brent, 'You're quite a philosopher,' for example, he's indulging in Socratic irony, highlighting the gaffer's cod philosophy. But Brent is us too, and his utterances contain something we would not be without. One particular moment, when Neil sits Brent down for the first of many tellings-off, perfectly captures the voice of the fool—the joker in the pack, the worker who doesn't quite work—as he laughs at and for us across the ages: 'David, when I was managing the Swindon branch, our perception of your branch was "They're having a laugh."' David's response? 'Thanks very much.'

# Chapter 6
# **Taking liberties**

DEREK: I tell you, the other day some bloke came up to me—I don't know who he was—and he said, 'You cunt.'...I said, 'You cunt,' I said, 'you fucking cunt,' I said, 'who are you fucking calling cunt, cunt?'

CLIVE: What'd he say to that?

DEREK: He said, 'You fucking cunt.'

> Dudley Moore and Peter Cook, *Derek and Clive (Live)*
> (1976)

## Biting, whipping, tickling

'Laughter is men's way of biting,' Baudelaire proclaimed. The sociologist Norbert Elias offered a rejoinder: 'He who laughs cannot bite.' So does laughter embody or diffuse aggression? One theory, offered by the neuroscientist Vilayanur Ramachandran, is that the laugh may be an aborted cry of concern, a way of announcing to a group that there has been a false alarm. The smile could operate in a similar way: when one of our ancestral primates saw another individual from a distance, he perhaps initially bared his canines as a threatening grimace before recognizing the individual as friend, not foe. So his grimace was abandoned halfway to produce a smile, which in turn may have evolved into a ritualized human greeting. Another researcher,

Robert Provine, notes that chimp laughter is commonly triggered by physical contact (biting or tickling) or by the threat of such contact (chasing games) and argues that the 'pant-pant' of apes and the 'ha-ha' of humans evolved from the breathlessness of physical play. This, together with the show of teeth necessitated by the play face, has been ritualized into the rhythmic pant of the laugh. Behind the smile, then, may lie a socialized snarl; and behind the laugh, a play fight. But behind both of these facial expressions lie real snarls and real fights.

People often claim to be 'only joking', but many a true word is spoken in jest. Ridicule and derision are both rooted in laughter (from *ridere*, to laugh). The comic may loiter with shady intent on the borders of aggression; 'a joke', Aristotle suggested, 'is a kind of abuse'. And comedy itself can be abused as well as used—racist and sexist jokes point to its potential cruelty. As Waters says of Price's stand-up act in Trevor Griffiths's *The Comedians* (1975): 'Love, care, concern, call it what you like, you junked it over the side.' Comedy is clearly at home in the company of insults, abuse, curses, and diatribes, but the mode can also lend an unusual inflection to these utterances. From Greek iambi to the licensed raillery of the Roman Saturnalia, from Pete and Dud on the implications of being called a fucking cunt to the game of The Dozens, in which numerous aspersions are cast upon Yo Mama's character, something strange happens to aggression when it is stylized or performed. W. H. Auden pondered choreographed exchanges of insult—from Old English flyting to the modern-day exchanges of truck drivers— and observed that 'the protagonists are not thinking about each other but about language and their pleasure in employing it inventively... Playful anger is intrinsically comic because, of all emotions, anger is the least compatible with play.' From this perspective, comedy is the moment at which outrage becomes outrageous. Some kinds of ferocity can be delectable.

'Playful anger' sounds like a contradiction in terms, yet in Plato's *Philebus*, Socrates notes 'the curious mixture of pleasure and pain that lies in the malice of amusement'. Descartes suggests in *The Passions of The Soul* (1649) that 'Derision or scorn is a sort of joy mingled with hatred.' This chapter examines such curious mixtures and minglings of feeling by considering modes of comedy that seem to have a target in their sights—versions of satire, mock-heroic, parody, and caricature. We might turn first to the satirist; Walter Benjamin identified him as 'the figure in whom the cannibal was received into civilization'. So the satirist is at once savage *and* civilized; he cuts us up after having been granted permission (perhaps even encouraged) to take that liberty. What is it, then, that we need this cannibal to do for us? The satirist, it would initially appear, is the comedian who allows audiences to join him on a mission. Satire is a scourge of vice, a spur to virtue; Horace imagines his ideal listener as 'baring his teeth in a grin'. So far so good, but the listener may also get bitten from time to time: 'What are you laughing at?' the poet asks us, 'Change the name and you are the subject of the story.' Indeed, as Hamlet would later quip, 'use every man after his desert, and who should scape whipping?'

In Juvenal's hands, satire begins as a revenger's comedy; his first satire opens: 'Must I always be a listener only, never hit back?' And yet his performances display such relish for repudiation that we may begin to wonder whether the mode is perhaps more inclined to whip than to improve the victim. Pursuing the Roman wives to their private chambers, he watches them take off their make-up to reveal . . . 'what shall we call it? A face, or an ulcer?' Ageing husbands don't fare any better: 'He has long forgotten what sex was like; if one tries to remind him, his shrunken tool, with its vein enlarged, just lies there, and, though caressed all night, it will continue to lie there.' The sheer élan of the enmity in Juvenal often gives the lie to any purported desire for change. Like his tools, the workmanlike victim must 'continue to lie there' and take it, if only to feed our pleasure in the continuance of the invective. The focus is less on recommending improvement or virtue, and more on revelling in the virtuosity of the attack.

The butt of the joke is an intermediary rather than an end point. In his fifteenth satire, Juvenal foreshadows Jonathan Swift's not so modest proposals when he turns to cases of cannibalism which, he says, may elicit 'anger, or in certain quarters possibly laughter'. As he explores the possible relations between 'hunger and hate', there arises the suspicion that the satirist-as-cannibal may himself hunger *to* hate, and that the *lanx satura* ('mixed dish') of satire creates a taste for what it claims to despise. A gruesome comedy is at work here, born of Juvenal's appreciation of the fact that disgust can be a kind of delight. John Dryden observed of the poet that 'his Spleen is raised, and he raises mine; I have the Pleasure of Concernment in all he says... he gives me as much Pleasure as I can bear'.

In some guises, perhaps, the 'Pleasure of Concernment' can slide into mere self-satisfaction, and the feeling that this pleasure is a guilty one raises a long-standing concern about comedy's gravitation towards insult and attack. The charge was put most clearly by Thomas Hobbes: 'laughter is nothing else but the sudden glory arising from some sudden conception of some eminency in ourselves, by comparison with the infirmity of others'. Hobbes's 'Superiority theory', and its accompanying emphasis on the cruelty of comic instincts, became the subject of much debate in the 18th century. Lord Shaftesbury countered that humour helps us to 'polish one another and rub off our corners and rough sides by a sort of amiable collision'. The philosopher Frances Hutcheson went further to develop what has come to be known as the 'Incongruity theory', claiming that a perceived 'incongruity' *in* a person, object or situation (rather than our sense of superiority *to* it) was the source of many kinds of laughter.

Alexander Pope has these discussions in mind when he observes that 'there is a difference betwixt laughing *about* a thing and laughing *at* a thing'. His mock-heroic poem *The Rape of the Lock* (1714) teases out the fineness of the distinction. Pope said that the poem was 'at once the most a satire, and the most inoffensive, of anything of mine. 'Tis a sort of writing very like tickling.' Hobbes's perspective meets and mingles with Hutcheson's: the satirist's superior slap, it turns out, is really a bit of slap and tickle, and tickling itself is an incongruous feeling, a mixture of pleasure and pain. As Adam Phillips ventures, tickling initiates us 'in a distinctive way into the helplessness and disarray of a certain primitive kind of pleasure'. This is not quite the security of Dryden's 'Pleasure of Concernment'; here, the pleasure is *in* the disarray, in our wish to be jostled a little. From one point of view, Pope's poem looks down on the vanities of polite society by narrating a petty squabble about Belinda's lock of hair in epic accents, implying that the domestic drama can't live up to heroic precedent. But the poem also raises a more ticklish subject, for the structural comparison doesn't only belittle the action. It also raises—and raises up—the quotidian details sometimes passed over by epic and suggests that they too merit our attention, perhaps even our regard. Aubrey Beardsley would capture both the glamour and the vanity of the scene in which Belinda prepares herself to meet the gentlemen (see Figure 13). Comedy is often a name we give to a space in which the admirable and the absurd can coexist. To 'humour' somebody, as Pope and Beardsley humour Belinda, is a way of enjoying their charms whilst also seizing on their limitations. The longevity of many comic forms is based on this fine line: to send something up is not necessarily—or not simply—to put it down.

## From protest to parody

The literary critic and theorist Kenneth Burke suggested that 'pure' humour is not protestant but acquiescent: 'A good humorist does not want to "make us go out and do something about it." Rather, he makes us feel, "Well, things may not be so bad after all. It all depends on how you look at them."' What, then, of those forms of humour that are tangled up in satires on the status quo? If satire is a criticism of things as they are, and if humour may

13. Aubrey Beardsley, 'The Toilette' (1896), illustration to Pope's *Rape of the Lock*

encourage tolerance of such things, are varieties of comic anger caught between the need to change the situation and the desire just to let off steam? Voltaire's *Candide* (1759) offers a way of thinking through these questions, for the book is itself a savage attack on the very inclination to say 'Well, things may not be so bad after all' (or, in Pangloss's pushier formulation, 'all is for the best'). Much of the brio of the story comes from the way in which this point of view is revealed as a cover story for complacency or heartlessness. Candide's question upon seeing his tutor hanged is still the right one: 'If this is the best of all possible worlds, what must the others be like?'

That said, one pleasure of reading Voltaire's prose comes from its seeming immunity to the suffering it encounters. Candide is 'flogged in cadence to the singing' of those who torture him; this might stand as shorthand for the comic unconcern of his author's style. The book deals with many losses—the forced loss of chastity, of innocence, of hope, of life—but the style itself is never at a loss. We read of mass stranglings and impalings, and learn that 'this catastrophe caused a great stir everywhere for several hours'. Several *hours*, not days or years. On finding out that his maiden Cunégonde is now mistress of another man, 'Candide was thunderstruck by this news; he wept for a long time; and at last he took Camambo aside...'. 'Wept for a long time'—but not quite long enough to merit a full stop. When Pangloss returns, having recovered from his hanging, he 'conceded that he had suffered horribly, all his life, but having once maintained that everything was going splendidly he would continue to do so, while believing nothing of the kind'. This is a final dig at the hypocrisy of the man's deterministic reading of the universe, but it's also an echo of the wickedly cool style of the book, for the statement is, in its way, a refusal to buckle under the pressure of circumstance or to admit defeat. Pangloss's whitewashing can be seen as a kind of stubborn effort. Perhaps comedy can teach you to be both a fatalist and a moralist at the same time.

In his *Philosophical Dictionary* (1764), Voltaire conceded his own attraction to fatalism, whilst also resisting the idea that this system of thought inevitably leads to indifference or apathy: 'I have *from necessity* the passion to write this; and you, you have the passion to contradict me: we are both equally foolish, equally the playthings of fate. Your nature is to do evil, mine is to love the truth and publish this in spite of you.' It sounds like Pangloss has been reincarnated as satirist. Voltaire's mixture of the blithe and the biting lies at the heart of many of the sharpest comebacks. A certain type of comic tone has continued to be shaped from such a passionate yet imperturbable calm; two hundred years later, when the composer and artist John Cage was asked, 'But don't you think there's too much suffering in the world?' he replied: 'No, I think there's just the right amount.' It is the question here, not the answer, which may be unthoughtful or even complacent. Cage speaks of an experience you have a right to feel—and, indeed, from which you may not always wish to be parted.

From Juvenal to Jon Stewart's *The Daily Show*, comedy across the ages has often been conceived and practised as an art of criticism, yet doubts have been raised about whether the mode does what it says on the tin. Does satire establish and defend a moral high ground, or make us unsure of whether such ground actually exists? Is it more difficult to disapprove of somebody if you find them ridiculous? Might laughing *at* somebody serve as an alibi for laughing *with* them—perhaps even laughing with them at yourself? Comic theatre has frequently put these questions with renewed force by suggesting to audiences that they share more than just a room with the characters they laugh at. Richard Sheridan's *The School for Scandal* (1777) is an exposure of a society that luxuriates in gossip, scandal, and spite, yet when Maria says of Lady Sneerwell and her cronies that 'Their malice is intolerable,' she is only half right. The playwright and audience are not just cocking a snook at malice, but playing the Peeping Tom. We may deride Mrs Candour's hypocrisy as she listens to the gossip—'Ha, ha, ha! Well, you make me laugh; but I vow I hate you for 't'—but she is our twin. The sheer sparkle of the malice is what we have come to listen to, and in this environment to be a witness is to be an accomplice.

What is heard in *The School for Scandal* is a recurrent tune in comedy, one in which a call to judgement can be finessed into a kind of pleasurable indulgence, or—more pointedly—into a questioning of our very need to *be* judgemental. In traditional comic theatre, most of the action occurred on the forestage, in front of the proscenium arch in a well-lit room (spectators were visible to each other and to the actors). This set-up heightened a sense of the audience as implicated addressees rather than as safely distanced spectators. According to Charles Lamb, the skill of the comic actor lay in those moments 'when, without absolutely appealing to an audience, he keeps up a tacit understanding with them…a perpetual sub-insinuation'. Such moments are central to comedy, and in Sheridan's play they tend to occur when the devilishly smooth-talking Joseph Surface glides onstage. Spectators judge Joseph at their peril, for when he says of Snake that 'the fellow hasn't virtue enough to be faithful even to his own villainy', a glance towards the audience offers a sub-insinuation about their own desire to dress up an appetite for villainy as a duty to watch plays for 'moral improvement'. If comedy is a force for good, it is so not because it paints definitive pictures of The Good Life, but because it challenges its audiences to entertain incongruous versions of what such a life might be.

Comedy has on many occasions taken shape not simply as a protest against vice, but as a reconsideration of what 'virtue' means. It makes ambiguous fun out of the idea that one particular style or writing or living has a monopoly on virtue (Jane Austen winningly confessed to her niece that 'Pictures of perfection, as you know, make me sick and wicked'). This is where the art of parodic doubling and impersonation comes into its own, an art that can shed further light on the strangely mercurial nature of comic mockery. Parody makes a 'mockery' of things in the full sense of the word: 'derision, ridicule', and also 'mimicry, imitation' (as one might 'mock up' a replica). The parodist often teases authors who have become self-regarding, yet imitation might also be a form of flattery, or at least a backhanded compliment. Parody can imply that the object is *worth* parodying; the mode is, after all, a parasite—a preserver, not just a destroyer. It needs and sustains its host. The authors of the *Bon Gaultier Ballads* (1845) took care to point out that 'it was precisely the poets whom we admired that we imitated most frequently. Let no one parody a poet unless he loves him.' Henry Reed felt this way about T. S. Eliot. Eliot's ruminations on time in 'Burnt Norton' (1936) led him to conclude the poem with the lines: 'Ridiculous the waste sad time | Stretching before and after.' In his parody, 'Chard Whitlow' (1941), Reed stretched things further by playing up the ridiculousness:

> As we get older we do not get any younger.
> Seasons return, and today I am fifty-five,
> And this time last year I was fifty-four,
> And this time next year I shall be sixty-two.

Reed inhabits as well as mocks Eliot's style and predicament. If the parodist here laughs at statements of the obvious, he also reminds us that the obvious has a habit of springing surprises. Call it the shock of the old.

The master of this parodic style of loving and laughing is Max Beerbohm, who defined caricature as the exaggeration of 'the peculiarities of a human being, at his most characteristic moment, in the most beautiful manner'. This is an apt description of Beerbohm's greatest parodies too (see Figure 14 and the accompanying text beneath it).

James was Beerbohm's favourite novelist, and both image and writing here pay homage as well as poke fun. The passage not only sounds like James, but also like an allegory of parody's peculiar operations: the mode can serve up a person's style with 'awful

26. London in November, and Mr Henry James in London. [c. 1907]
...It was, therefore, not without something of a shock that he, in this to him so very congenial atmosphere, now perceived that a vision of the hand which he had, at a venture, held up within an inch or so of his eyes was, with an almost awful clarity being adumbrated . . .

**14. Max Beerbohm, 'London in November and Mr Henry James in London' (c.1907)**

clarity' whilst providing a 'congenial atmosphere' in which to do
so. Suddenly shocked by himself, translated into something rich
and strange, the subject is at his most 'characteristic' moment
rendered comically, incongruously peculiar to himself.

James was delighted by Beerbohm's takes on his style, acknowledging that, whenever he now wrote, he felt he was 'parodying himself'. Although parodists are often keen to make fun out of their subjects, they also draw attention to the fun that might be had within them, taking their cue from the comedy that lies half-hidden in the original. Run-of-the-mill parody is a kind of irony—the mimicking of a style or a sentiment without really 'meaning' it—but the best parody is replete with a more complex type of ironic tone, one that is present in the subterranean humour of James's own late style. It's what Spencer Brydon appreciates in Alice Staverton in *The Jolly Corner* (1908): 'Her smile had for him, with the words, the particular mild irony with which he found half her talk suffused; an irony without bitterness and that came, exactly, from her having so much imagination.' Many comic talents have nurtured this kind of irony. It suggests that criticism can be a form of collusion, and that we take the biggest liberties with those we care about the most. In this guise, comedy is a story of how taunting becomes teasing becomes treasuring.

## Anything goes

But how can this story be squared with the bracing energy of other kinds of comic contempt? Some versions of comedy may point to a consensus of values that stands secure beneath differences of opinion and outlook, yet our strongest laughter isn't always of the warm and fuzzy variety. Evelyn Waugh provides an antidote to tender feeling with an irony that's more wild than mild. He acknowledged that satire 'flourishes in a stable society and presupposes homogenous moral standards. It exposes polite cruelty and folly.' However, for Waugh, in the modern age, 'vice no longer pays lip service to virtue'. So if we're all going to the dogs, there's no call—and no hope—for satirical business as usual. Something weirder is required. Perhaps a kind of heartless elation may flower in such a wasteland.

At the opening of Waugh's first novel, *Decline and Fall* (1928), the larks at the Bollinger Club are recalled with fondness: 'At the last dinner, three years ago, a fox had been brought in in a cage and stoned to death with champagne bottles. What an evening that had been!' This is more vertiginously, comically delightful than just a satire on the bottle-throwers (satire is often a way of saying that you care, but in Waugh's fiction caring is itself satirized). Later a young lad is accidentally shot in the foot: '"Am I going to die?" said Tangent, his mouth full of cake.' Then he has the foot amputated, and then he dies, but so what? '"Oh death, where is thy sting-a-ling-a-ling," said the surgeon.' It's as though the writing has pushed through anger, or pity, or sorrow, and come out the other side. Praising Waugh in relation to 'his great precursor, Juvenal', Gore Vidal glimpsed the heart of the matter: 'at full strength, wit is rage made bearable'.

To put it this way is to suggest that a genius for comedy like Waugh's suffers not from lack of feeling, but rather delights in a plenitude of feeling *staged* as a lack. In *The Ordeal of Gilbert Pinfold* (1957), Waugh's fictionalized self explains that 'he wished no one ill, but he looked at the world *sub specie aeternitatis* and he found it flat as a map; except when, rather often, personal annoyance intruded. Then he would come tumbling from his exalted point of observation.' Recall Hobbes's definition of the reason for laughter, but this time note his crucial rider: a 'sudden conception of some eminency in ourselves, by comparison with the infirmity of others, *or with our own formerly*' (my italics). Pinfold's tumble into humanity (and also into temporary insanity) suggests that the most uncaring kind of ridicule (the *sub specie aeternitatis* kind) is sometimes an attempt to ward off one's own fear of being compromised. Martin Amis has claimed that 'all good satire is complicit with what it exposes', and as Pinfold will discover when he starts to hear persecutory voices, it takes one to know one. Demonization of others can be a way of placating inner demons. You project your own secret vices or wishes onto others, get vicarious gratification from watching them indulge in shady pleasures, before then punishing them for it. As a way of gleaning pleasure from pain, and of teasing revelry out of rage, comedy has frequently been at ease around sadomasochism. Some of the funniest moments in Waugh's novel come when the protagonist stages an ambush for the imagined voices and people inside his head: 'He would fell the first with his blackthorn, then change this weapon for the malacca cane. The second young man no doubt would stumble over his fallen friend. Mr Pinfold would then turn on the light and carefully thrash him.' Carefully does it, or you might do yourself an injury.

This reading of Pinfold's little psychodrama still holds to the idea that there's a method in the madness (perverse as that method may be), but comedy can go further than this, sabotaging its own agendas by committing to a kind of anarchic glee. Take *The Simpsons*, for example, which is both satire and a step beyond it. The show is liberally sprinkled with attacks on the corruption of the authorities and authority figures—be it Mr Burns, Police Chief Wiggam, Mayor Quimby, or even Rupert Murdoch and the show's own sister channel, Fox News (one episode in 2010 opened with a Fox helicopter sporting a new slogan: 'Not Racist, But #1 With Racists'). But it's not only the big guys who indulge in shameless behaviour; the little guys are at it too. Lisa praises her dad for becoming president of the workers' union: 'This is your chance to get a fair shake for the working man.' Homer completes the thought: 'And to make lifelong connections to the world of organized crime.' 'Mmmm,' he murmurs, just as he would over a Duff Beer, 'Organized crime.' Like the show itself, and like his father, Bart sometimes delights in depravity just for the hell of it—a depravity we enjoy rather than judge. In one episode Bart sells his soul to Milhouse for $5; when Lisa complains that the figure is a pittance, her brother chuckles: 'Well, if you think he got such a good deal, I'll sell you my conscience for $4.50.' Lisa will later remind Bart that 'Pablo Neruda said laughter is the language of the soul' (Bart replies with panache: 'I am familiar with the works of Pablo Neruda'). But the laughter the kids have in mind is not angelic; it's a devilishly dark, unhinged laughter, one which cackles at the violence of *The Itchy and Scratchy Show*, or at Homer doubled over in pain after falling victim to a practical joke. Bart can't take pleasure in these things until he gets back his soul at the end of the episode; the last scene features both the boy and his soul laughing in wild joy at the thought of a world that remains subject to malevolence and misadventure.

'I want to be evil,' Eartha Kitt deliciously sings: 'Like something that seeks its level, | I wanna go to the devil.' Anybody who has heard the sound of Bart's laughter knows that some comic instincts revel in crimes and misdemeanors because...well, just because. Call it Bart for Bart's sake. As he says elsewhere: 'I don't know! I don't know why I did it, I don't know why I enjoyed it, and I don't know why I'll do it again!' Like bad behaviour, comedy often feels so wrong it's right. Take the gag that is lovingly recounted by dozens of comedians in the documentary *The Aristocrats* (2005). There isn't space to retell it here, but it's nothing too scandalous—just the usual tale of a family that goes in for a spot of incest, necrophilia, bestiality, and other hobbies. People don't just eat shit in this joke, they gargle with it, and the story exists to give obscene, triumphant expression to whatever it is in us that wants to say or imagine things we shouldn't. The stand-up George Carlin, who tells the joke particularly well, observes more generally: 'I do like finding out where the line is drawn, deliberately crossing it, bringing some of the audience with me across the line, and having them be happy that I did.' That happiness is hard to account for, but it's perhaps got something to do with the feeling that comedy can momentarily allow us to inhabit a world without shame, a world in which we are free from the pressure of needing to worry about causing or taking offence.

'The aim of a joke is not to degrade the human being, but to remind him that he is already degraded,' George Orwell said. Hobbes's followers would have it that we laugh at what is odd in order to get even, that we use jokes to police communities and to create scapegoats. This is certainly true, but Orwell's comment points to another truth: the feeling—notwithstanding the superiority of the joker who is issuing the reminder—that we are all in the same boat (which may be sinking). The poet-critic Geoffrey Grigson claims that 'one can gravely say that satire postulates an ideal condition of man or decency, and then despairs of it; and enjoys the despair, masochistically'. From this perspective, comedy might be read as a satire upon the vanity of human wishes and as a reminder of our degradation, but the reminder itself can be a way of excusing—and enjoying—our weaknesses. Grigson said it gravely, but the humorist Jack Handey provides a good comic translation, one which Bart Simpson would like: 'I can picture in my mind a world without war, a world without hate. And I can picture us attacking that world, because they'd never expect it.'

# Chapter 7
# Beyond a joke

Although what I have basically been doing about the rain is
ignoring it, to tell the truth.

How I do that is by walking in it.

David Markson, *Wittgenstein's Mistress* (1988)

## What's so funny?

Comedy is not always a laughing matter. Hamlet is shocked that
one of the gravediggers sees fit to crack jokes: 'Has this fellow no
feeling at his business, that he sings at grave-making?' Yet the
hero himself whistles in the dark as his tragedy unfolds, not least
here, when he dwells on the skull of poor Yorick, once 'a fellow of
infinite jest', whom Hamlet now describes as 'quite chop-fallen'.
Chin up. If this is funny, why isn't it funnier? Perhaps because we
sense that the prince is reaching for comedy to get himself
through the day. Thinking about what goes into such achievement,
Flann O'Brien was drawn to such interludes—comic relief as the
comedy *of* relief—noting that Joyce shared with Shakespeare an
understanding of humour as 'the handmaid of sorrow and
fear...true humour needs background urgency'. It not only needs
it, but needs to do something with it, acknowledging it whilst also
turning sorrow and fear into an aside. Take two examples. From
O'Brien's *The Third Policeman* (1939–40): 'I broke my left leg (or,

if you like, it was broken for me) in six places'; and from Vladimir Nabokov's *Lolita* (1955): 'My very photogenic mother died in a freak accident (picnic, lightning) when I was three.' The parentheses put trauma in its place, but they also stand as comedy's awareness of the fact that trauma *has* a place.

For Hamlet, Humbert Humbert, and many others, comedy has been something that comes to the rescue. As Leopold Bloom thinks to himself in *Ulysses* (1922), 'You must laugh sometimes so better do it that way. Gravediggers in *Hamlet*. Shows the profound knowledge of the human heart.' Stephen Daedalus shares this feeling for comedy as a way of trying to dig yourself out of a hole. When he expounds his theory on Shakespeare (and his own version of himself as Hamlet), it feels apt that he should find space to laugh at his predicament: 'He laughed to free his mind from his mind's bondage.' If you were to ask a comic character, 'Do you laugh?' the answer would frequently come back: 'Only when it hurts.' Nietzsche proclaimed: 'Perhaps I know best why man alone laughs. He alone suffers so deeply that he had to invent laughter.' The blithe leap from first to third person here is part of the seriousness of the joke; like the laugh, the quip is a way of expressing and backing off from the speaker's own suffering. Others have sympathized with this Nietzschean way of knowing: in his *Anatomy of Melancholy* (1621), Robert Burton cited many authorities who supported his view that laughter occurs most often in melancholy people; William Blake's *Marriage of Heaven and Hell* (1790–3) informs us that 'excess of sorrow laughs'; and in Joyce's *Finnegans Wake* (1939) man suffers so much that he has to invent a new word to describe how he feels: 'laughtears'.

The most developed theory of how and why laughter is shadowed by seriousness is Freud's. Or rather, he has two theories. In *The Joke and Its Relation to the Unconscious*, he writes that 'Through our culture's work of repression, primary possibilities of enjoyment, now spurned by the censorship within us, are lost.' A joke, like a dream, is a surreptitious reclaiming of that enjoyment, a disguised way of relieving the pain caused by repressing forbidden desires. It's the id's way of sneaking though our conscious defences: 'we can only laugh when the joke has come to our help'. In his later essay on 'Humour', though, Freud ponders the criminal led to the gallows on a Monday morning who says: 'Well, that's a good start to the week.' In Freud's view, this kind of comic turn means: 'Look, this is the world that looks so dangerous. It is child's play, it is only right to make a joke about it!' So the id is no longer the main player. This is the realm of the conscientious superego, which 'strives to comfort the ego through humour, and to protect it from suffering'. Now the joke is shaped by the loving parent, whereas before it was under the sway of the imp of the perverse. Civilized protector has taken the place of unconscious desirer, although in both scenarios the comic impulse is being conceived as a response to pain and as a mode of coping. This chapter considers the wide range of shapes that such responses can take, and asks: what might follow from comedy's being seen as both the avoidance and the expression of life's darker sides—as civilization *and* its discontents?

Memorable definitions of comedy have been hewn out of its apparent opposition to tragedy: 'The world is a comedy to those that think, and tragedy to those that feel' (Horace Walpole); 'Comedy is life viewed from a distance; tragedy, life in close-up' (Charlie Chaplin); 'Tragedy is when I cut my little finger. Comedy is when you fall into an open sewer and die' (Mel Brooks). All revel in the sense of comedy as a detached perspective, yet from way back it was felt that comedy and tragedy were not quite true opposites. Plato's *Symposium* closes with Socrates asking two exemplars of the rival modes (Aristophanes and Agathon) to concede that 'the genius of comedy was the same as that of tragedy, and that the true artist in tragedy was an artist in comedy also. To this they were constrained to assent, being drowsy, and not quite following the argument.' The argument has not yet been settled, but Christopher Fry has offered a productive way of staging it: 'when I first set about writing a comedy the idea presents itself to me first of all as a tragedy,' he explains. 'If the characters were not qualified for tragedy, there would be no comedy, and to some extent I have to cross the one before I can get to the other.' Perhaps tragedy and comedy are more alike than they are supposed to be. Indeed, we might wonder why people have so often felt the need to keep them separate.

Comedy does not preclude tragedy; it presupposes it. In Aristophanes's *The Acharnians*, when Dicaeopolis says that 'comedy has a sense of duty too', the Greek word for 'comedy' in this line is not the usual *komoidia*, but *trugoidia* ('goat-song', 'trygedy'), with the pun suggesting that comic energies dance on tragic ground. The earliest comic fragments to have survived are parodies of Homer, and Greek tragedians originally submitted their plays as a tetralogy: the first three plays were tragedies, and the fourth was an afterpiece—a satyr play—which offered a burlesque of some aspect of the preceding triad. So the satyr play occupied a middle ground between tragedy and comedy. Euripides's *Cyclops* (*c.*408 BC) provides a farcical take on the scene in Homer's *Odyssey* where Odysseus blinds Polyphemus in order to save his men and make his escape. In Euripides, the hero's role is to free Silenus and his Dionysian crew from Polyphemus's clutches, but in this retelling the villain is given lines which make humour out of hubris: 'If Zeus thunders at me,' Polyphemus explains, 'I wank in his face.' 'You'll go blind,' the gods might reply. After Polyphemus's own face has suffered an indignity, the satyr chorus stays back to toy with him by playing blind man's buff: 'You're mocking me,' he laments 'I'm just a butt.' It's an odd moment. The critic and translator Stephen Halliwell asks good questions of it: 'Has Euripides deflated an originally horrifying myth to the status of a blindfold children's game, or followed through the logic of the taunting laughter of victimisation?' The play seems to offer reassurance—'no real Cyclops was harmed during the making of this drama'—yet at the same time draws out our sympathy for the victim. If, as Max Eastman claimed, 'humour is the instinct for taking pain playfully', then it should be added that comedy is often drawn to a consideration of the very peculiarity of this instinct.

## Mixed feelings

Comedy's enduring interest in pain—and its need to withstand it—receives one of its greatest expressions in Cervantes's *Don Quixote* (1605–15). The Knight of the Sorrowful Countenance takes so much physical abuse and mental torture that some artists have shied away from depicting the suffering which resides in his face (see Figure 15).

**15. Honoré Daumier, 'Don Quixote' (1868)**

Yet Daumier's painting is only following Quixote's lead, for the self-created knight errant often refuses to look at himself and his world head-on. In this sense, Quixote is an embodiment of comedy's frequent resistance to reality. When Sancho Panza reminds his master that it's all make-believe, Quixote is adamant: 'I want you to realize that all the things I am doing are not jokes but very real.' This avoidance of 'the real' *is* the joke upon which the novel is built, and yet at many points in the book the make-believe turns real (as the narrator points out of the actors, 'they seemed to have been transformed into the very parts they were playing'). Although we humour Quixote because we sense that he needs to be in his own little world to avoid his suffering, it gradually dawns on us that this world is a large-minded creation. It's as though the comedy set out to laugh at delusion before turning the joke on those who insist on staying sober (something like Robin Williams's feeling that 'reality is just a crutch for people who can't cope with drugs').

This one-liner underplays the reach of comedies like Cervantes's, though, because what looks like escapism or cowardice in Quixote is also a kind of bravery and a commitment to idealism (he notes of another person's duplicities that 'they cannot and should not be called deceptions, since their purpose was virtuous'). Quixote is one of comedy's representative heroes because he reminds us that those lacking in imagination can be *too* healthy. Whilst acknowledging the dangers of losing one's grip on reality, the psychoanalyst D. W. Winnicott observed that 'there are others who are so firmly anchored in objectively perceived reality that they are ill in the opposite direction of being out of touch with the subjective world and with the creative approach to fact'. Quixote is a vital reminder of the sheer amount of wish fulfilment that goes into the making of a life—and of the fact that you could become estranged from your life by relinquishing fantasy. From this perspective, comedy is born from a sense of the truth in fabulation.

It may seem laughable to reimagine a local peasant girl you have a crush on as Dulcinea del Toboso, but such an exaggerated

write-up of the beloved is not, after all, so very unus⟨ual⟩
is put to him that Dulcinea is just an illusory image⟨ of the⟩
perfection he craves, Quixote's reply is in a perfectl⟨y⟩
comic key, for it shows how an apparent avoidance ⟨of⟩
questions could be the route to a wisdom which should be
cherished: 'There is much to say about that…these are not
the kinds of things whose verification can be carried through to
the end.' The comic butt frequently stands accused of wishful
thinking, yet this thinking is also part of the larger power of
comedy, which as a mode tends to acknowledge that there is
much more to say even while it sticks to its story. The pathos we
encounter in Don Quixote and his comic successors is not quite
the denial of pain, but rather the unwillingness to have it
explicitly verified. We admire and pity him the more because he
refuses to have pity for himself.

There are darker versions of comedy's dealings with pain than
this, of course, ones that make the risible and the resilient even
stranger bedfellows. The narrator of Jonathan Swift's *A Tale of a
Tub* (1704) lays out the challenge in one gorgeous sentence: 'Last
Week I saw a Woman flay'd, and you will hardly believe how
much it altered her Person for the worse.' In his anthology and
defence of *Black Humour* (1940), André Breton saw Swift as the
mode's true initiator, a mode which is 'the mortal enemy of
sentimentality'. But not necessarily, it should be said, the enemy
of sentiment. Taking the prose joyfully out of context, the thrill of
Swift's sentence comes from the fact that the writer could trust
enough to our sensibilities to risk putting the thing down on
paper. Something similar occurs when the narrator of Swift's
*A Modest Proposal* (1729) argues that the Irish paupers should
sell their babies as foodstuffs in order to ease their troubles. This
is meant as a satire on the brutality of the Hanoverian
establishment that was devouring Ireland, but the victims are not
themselves spared the lash. Under the scheme, it is anticipated,
parents would try to bring 'the fattest child to market',
which would mean that 'Men would become as fond of their

, during the time of their pregnancy, as they are now of their
[ma]res in foal, their cows in calf, or sow when they are ready to
[f]arrow; nor offer to beat or kick them (as is too frequent a
practice) for fear of a miscarriage.' So babies would be raised,
rather than lowered, to the status of beasts, and wives—promoted
to cattle—would finally get handled with care. O brave new
world, that has such people in it.

Such deadpan ironies can make comedy the defender of the finer
feelings against which it offends. Perhaps it even elicits these
feelings in the reader by affecting to disregard them. Yet a
vertiginous comic energy like Swift's often seems to thrive on the
difficulty of our knowing how to take it, of our wondering whether
it doesn't perhaps partake of the callousness it anatomizes. In
*Thoughts on Various Subjects* (1706), Swift noted: 'If a man will
observe as he walks the streets, I believe he will find the merriest
countenances in mourning coaches.' This leaves it archly
undecided as to whether the mourners *need* the merriment to get
them through their mourning, or whether they are there merely
for show (simply glad to see the back of their dearly departed).
Likewise with the blithe narrator who casually walks the streets
observing such things: does he care, or does he not? Swift once
described human life as 'a ridiculous tragedy, which is the worst
kind of composition'. A dark comedy may be the best answer one
can muster when faced by this messy state of affairs. Any single
life should be taken seriously, but not too seriously.

Comedy has on many occasions aimed for a vantage point from
which it can dwell on passion. In the 19th and 20th centuries, this
balancing of detachment and engagement became a formative
influence on how the category of the humorous was theorized and
discussed: Arthur Schopenhauer, for example, defines humour as
'the seriousness concealed behind a joke', while Luigi Pirandello
claims that humour is *'the feeling of the opposite* ... almost a mirror
in which feeling looks at itself'. Modern comedy often stages
mixed feelings about feelings themselves. Alexander Pushkin's

*Eugene Onegin* (1825–32) is founded on this dialectic. On the one hand, it shares the amusement of many of those people who don't seem to be troubled by feeling, seem to be emptied of them—Onegin is gently mocked for emotions 'from outside', as if he weren't himself an earthling. On the other hand, the narrator himself lives a semi-detached kind of life, intuitively grasping a recurring demand of the comic imagination: its bid for exemption from feeling. Men are merely 'instruments and tools; | feeling is quaint, and fit for fools'; 'Friendship, as I must own to you, | blooms when there's nothing else to do.' The humour comes from a tone that flirts with ruefulness without quite submitting to it. There is seriousness concealed behind the joke ('how tiring, that life should be as tiresome as this'), but the exquisite artifice of the couplet also palliates the flatness it describes.

The search for comedy amid unpromising materials—the feeling that humour may lurk in the humdrum—is pushed to its most fantastical extreme by Nikolai Gogol, whom Pushkin praised for 'presenting the banality of life so vividly'. Gogol sharpens his wit on banality and its close relations. In his hands, the trite, the drab, the trumped-up, and the not-worth-talking-about become a means of excited discovery. 'The comic is concealed everywhere,' Gogol writes, 'living in its midst we do not see it.' For him, the comic is itself an appreciation of how the quotidian can turn mysteriously luminous. In *Dead Souls* (1842), a page is spent observing Selifan scratching his head: 'God knows, there's no guessing. Many and various among the Russian people are the meanings of scratching one's head.' Later on the narrator reorients us: 'So here we are again in the backwoods, again we have come out in some corner! Yes, but what a backwoods and what a corner!' Everywhere, it seems, plenitude is observed in pettiness: 'To such worthlessness, pettiness, vileness a man can descend! So changed he can become! Does this resemble the truth? Everything resembles the truth, everything can happen to a man.' Even while Gogol is dressing down his characters for their insipid es, his style is dressing them up and delighting in them, as en he catches the protagonist Chichikov poring over his own image—and that of his new suit—in the mirror: 'Such a fool, but, overall, what a picture he makes!' Recall Pirandello's understanding of humour as 'almost a mirror in which feeling looks at itself'. In this guise, comedy is a kind of second glance, a moment in which somebody is caught hold of—or catches hold of themselves—as trivial yet also as larger than life. Chichikov's feelings are laughable, but they are not disavowed.

## Putting on a brave face

Dark comedies like grey areas. They play and prey upon lives which seem to be lacking something (that would be *all* lives, then) and make us unsure of how we are meant to be taking them. Theatrical art can heighten the ambiguity because, as members of an audience, we are prompted to consider our own laughs and sighs in relation to those we hear around us. Anton Chekhov's plays think through the implications of this. Although they've often been staged and performed as tragedies, the playwright was adamant they were not: 'A Comedy in Four Acts' was his subtitle for both *The Seagull* (1896) and *The Cherry Orchard* (1904), and he also described the latter as 'a four-act vaudeville' and 'farce'. Chekhov started off as a writer of comic sketches and vaudeville turns. In *The Bear* (subtitled 'A Joke in One Act') (1888), Popova vows fidelity to the memory of her late husband, continually moaning, 'my love will never die', before then threatening to kill the first man that comes her way, before then crying out, 'go, go! I hate the sight of you! Or no…Don't go.…Get away from me! Take your hands off me! I hate you! I demand satisfaction! [*A prolonged kiss*]'. The hypochondriacs, the luxuriatingly lonesome, the angst-ridden—why are such people so funny? Because making too much of pain only makes light of it, and because if someone has that much self-pity to spare, then we think they're probably in a safe enough place. The heart-on-his-sleeve suitor in *The Proposal* (1888–9) is happy indeed as he screams and swoons: 'I'm having a heart attack! My shoulder's missing! Where's my shoulder? I'm dying!'

The subterranean humour of Chekhov's later work owes something to these early dalliances, but in the later plays—as so often in great comedy—the humour relies on the gravity of what it makes into fun. These are plays that make us wonder what, exactly, we are getting when we 'get' a joke. The opening words of *The Seagull* are given to Medvedenko, who asks Masha, 'Why do you always wear black?' Hamlet-like, she replies, 'I'm in mourning for my life.' This line may get laughs, but they are probably uneasy ones, for Masha is still living with her emotion as well as casting ironic side glances at it. Later, Dorn sighs, 'Youth, youth!' and Masha observes: 'Whenever there's nothing more to be said then people say: "Youth, youth…"' [*Takes a pinch of snuff*]'. Comedy puts sadness into quotation marks not because it lacks feeling, but because it needs to frame it in order to keep the show on the road. When, in *The Cherry Orchard*, Lyubov oscillates wildly between 'Laugh at me, I'm such a fool' and 'There's nothing funny in the world,' she summarizes the range of responses the play calls forth in us, a play in which figures of fun are turned so calmly, coolly in the light that it can be hard to keep watching.

You can't *not* laugh when Lyubov's brother Gayev talks to the furniture in the first act—'Dear bookcase! Most esteemed bookcase! I salute your existence'—but he does so because the bookcase seems solid and dependable whilst the family's world crumbles around it, and because it is dawning on him that the bookcase is on its way out too. For Chekhov, comedy becomes a way of understanding the complexity of a life by refusing to pronounce judgement on it. On the notion that you could divide people up into 'successful' and 'unsuccessful' types, he once wrote to a friend: 'Are you successful or aren't you? What about me? What about Napoleon? One would need to be a god to distinguish successful from unsuccessful people without making mistakes. I'm going to a dance.' Recalling Chaplin's formulation on tragedy and comedy, we might say that this is life viewed in close-up but with a sense of distance helping to clarify that view. Chekhov's questions alone tell of his far-sightedness; they remind us that comedy's gaze can be both precise and panoramic.

The trees come down in the cherry orchard to make way for an even bleaker comic landscape. 'The essential achievement of modern art,' explained Thomas Mann, 'is that it has ceased to recognize the categories of the tragic and the comic...and sees life as tragicomedy.' Tragicomedy is older than this comment might imply (Plautus coined the word in the prologue to his *Amphitryon* in around 190 BC), but there's no doubt that modern art has made this mixed-up sense of life its special province. Henrik Ibsen and August Strindberg chose the term 'tragicomedy' when describing their plays *The Wild Duck* (1884) and *Creditors* (1889), as did Samuel Beckett in his subtitle for the English version of *Waiting For Godot* (1955). In Beckett's *Watt* (1953), we hear of the 'the laugh of laughs, the *risus purus*...the laugh that laughs—silence please—at that which is unhappy.' This is the kernel of tragicomedy. Nell points out in Beckett's *Endgame* (1957) that 'Nothing is funnier than unhappiness, I grant you that. Yes, yes, it's the most comical thing in the world' (Beckett noted: 'That for me is the most important sentence in the play'). Unhappiness is often comical in Beckett's world because of the way in which people stage their unhappiness *as* important, as though they assumed they had a right to happiness. Self-pity becomes a form of ludicrous self-righteousness, and despair a flair for masochism. Yet these connoisseurs of misery take on a battered nobility as they become aware of their plight and begin to play with it. Their jokes offer a way of living with unhappiness—and possibly through it.

Tragicomedy starts from the place where there is, as the first words of *Waiting for Godot* put it, 'Nothing to be done.' But the stage direction that accompanies the words is important too, for Estragon, we learn, is '*Giving up again*'. Ah...*again*. This is the heartbeat of the comedy of the absurd, and it's present in much of Beckett's writing—from the final words of *The Unnamable* (1953), 'you must go on, I can't go on, I'll go on', to the title of *Imagination Dead Imagine* (1965) and beyond. Thomas Nagel sees the absurd as a three-stage drama: armed with ideals, policing yourself with purposes, you are leading your life (or, rather, *pursuing* it); then, suddenly, you are caught off guard by a sense of your life's idiocy, or triviality, or futility; and then, since you cannot do very much as a mere spectator of your life, you go back to living it. Man, says Nagel, is 'full of doubts he is unable to answer, but also full of purposes he is unable to abandon'. So our very sense of the absurd is an achievement because it shows that we are able to transcend ourselves in thought, yet also a predicament because it seems to involve falling into old mistakes in new ways. Beckett's *Molloy* (1955) intones: 'My life, my life, now I speak of it as something over, now as of a joke which still goes on.' It sounds like expectation is a practical joke you play on yourself. In *Endgame*, Clov asks Hamm, 'Do you believe in the life to come?' Hamm: 'Mine was always that.' He is the archetypal tragicomic hero, somebody who keeps on with the comedy of errors, somebody on the lookout for fertile expedients whilst he conducts futile experiments. This form of comedy is a commitment to improvising with suffering rather than succumbing to it, and to failing again, failing better. In 1935, Beckett reported to a friend: 'Miss Costello said to me "You haven't a good word to say for anyone but the failures." I thought that was quite the nicest thing anyone had said to me for a long time.'

'Life does not cease to be funny when people die any more than it ceases to be serious when people laugh,' notes Ridgeon in George Bernard Shaw's *The Doctor's Dilemma* (1906). So perhaps we can end by returning to those seriously funny 'laughtears'. When considering laughter's relationship to crying, the philosopher and sociologist Helmuth Plessner observed that both actions are 'a response to a situation...from which we step back without really wishing to free ourselves from it'. Laughter arises from situations that are somehow 'unanswerable', so 'Man answers directly with laughter, without implicating himself in the answer.' But perhaps the laughter *is* the way we're implicated; this is not the promise of catharsis through comedy, but rather the gainsaying of a situation without denying it. Not exactly an answer, then, but rather a posing of the question in a way that makes it feel less threatening through our very ability to pose it so clearly (see Figure 16).

16. Saul Steinberg, from *The Inspector* (1973)

Comedy has often been an apprehension of life itself as a Sisyphean labour, but with some of the apprehension taken out. Geoffrey Willans's and Ronald Searle's Molesworth books (1953–9) are shadowed by their hero's question, 'Wots the use?' After all, 'look at the world it is worse than big skool ... And yet it still go on.' And Molesworth will go on too. He is a kind of comic Hamlet. He knows that something is rotten in the state of St Custard's but he isn't going to let that stop him: 'It is time i took over. I can see it all.' 'To be or not to be?' is a question that can lead to tragedy (and, in Hamlet's case, it says that tragedy has already occurred). But from Molesworth's 'Wots the use?' to Ernst Lubitsch's *To Be or Not to Be* (1942) to further back in time, the interrogative mode of the darkest, most delightful comedy usually receives a response which, whilst giving the question its due, also takes it with a pinch of salt. To be or not to be: that is not *the* question, but it is *a* question. 'There are moments, Jeeves, when one asks oneself "Do trousers matter?"' Bertie sighs woefully in P. G. Wodehouse's *The Code of the Woosters* (1938). 'The mood will pass, sir.' It will indeed pass, as will we all. In the meantime, though, best get dressed.

# Chapter 8
# Endgames

NILES: I hardly need to tell you how the story ends.

FRASIER: Just tell me *when* the story ends.

*Frasier* (1997)

## Corpsing

Comic endings can be a last laugh and a last resort. 'Die, my dear? Why, that's the last thing I'll do!' Groucho Marx is reputed to have said as he passed away. Famous last words often turn a quandary into an achievement; Dylan Thomas signed out by noting 'I've had eighteen straight whiskies. I think that's a record.' Apocryphal or not, this is what we would like him to have said. Even those who refuse to play by the rules of the game stay in tune with its spirit. When Karl Marx was asked by his housekeeper if he had any advice for posterity, he replied: 'Go on, get out! Last words are for fools who haven't said enough.' Yet these too are last words. The speaker goes out with a bang, not with a whimper; the utterance is close enough to aphorism to make it feel like the best is being made of a bad situation. Endings like this are at the centre of the human comedy because they play up the folly of it all while playing down the sadness which informs that folly. Montaigne claimed that 'my natural style is that of comedy', and what this style finally arrives at is a luminous sense of the oddity of how we're all placed: 'Our own specific property,' the essayist wrote, 'is to be equally laughable and able to laugh.'

Dying words sketch out one way that comedy handles endings: as a coming to terms with life, with limitation, with mortality, but on terms which make the sense of an ending more bearable. Yet some instincts refuse to be laid to rest, and voices from beyond the grave speak of another feature of the comic impulse: somewhere deep within comedy there lies the idea of not wanting to stop. In Aristophanes's *Frogs*, Dionysus tries to strike a deal with a corpse who is crossing the Styx:

DIONYSUS: How would you like to take my baggage to hell?
CORPSE: Two drachmas up front, or no deal.
DIONYSUS [*counting his change*]: I've got... nine obols. What do you say?
CORPSE: I'd sooner live again! [*He lies down again with a jerk.*]

The comedy lies not just in the thrill of feeling that life has been put in its place, but also in the awareness that there's plenty of life in this old dog yet. The corpse's recalcitrance commits him to the vitality he disdains.

Freud observed that 'Our own death is indeed unimaginable, and whenever we make the attempt to imagine it we can perceive that we really survive as spectators.' Comedy has frequently been drawn to this survival. Moving from last words to epitaphs, we hear a recurring refrain: 'Life is a jest; and all things show it. | I thought so once; but now I know it' (John Gay, 'My Own Epitaph', 1732). And the 'I' lives on in knowing it, in a 'now' that keeps things going. Similarly with Spike Milligan's epitaph: 'I told you I was ill.' Comedy as a P. S., as a desire to say 'And another thing...', is often an insistence that good things do *not* come to an end. Comic endings always seem to imply a future. When Mark Twain noted that 'reports of my death have been greatly exaggerated' he hit upon a good epitaph for comedy, for the mode suggests that death as the final outcome is itself something of an exaggeration. This chapter takes on endings as a way of considering the ends of the comedy more generally. I'll look at two varieties of endgame—the first eschatological (comedy's relationship with death, religion, and the afterlife) and the second sublunary (comedy's gravitation towards romance, marriage, and happy ever afters).

## Last things

Christ's own last utterance is a good place to begin: 'It is finished.' 'What is finished?' Christina Rossetti asked in her poem 'Amen'. Alfred Tennyson saw the cry as 'the most pathetic utterance in all history'; nevertheless, the poet's son reported, 'he also recognized the note of triumph'. Maybe the poet felt that Christ was expiring on a pun, eking out the triumph of 'All has come to fruition' from the pathos of 'The pain is finally ending.' Much has been made of the fact that Jesus is reported three times to have wept yet never to have laughed, but the contours of the Christian story are themselves shaped by the movement from tears to laughter, as Jesus explained: 'Blessed are ye that weep now: for ye shall laugh' (Luke 6:21). 'It is finished' may contain a similar confidence about last things. Northrop Frye claimed that 'the sense of tragedy as a prelude to comedy is hardly separable from anything explicitly Christian...The ritual pattern behind the catharsis of comedy is the resurrection that follows death.' This kind of resurrection brings into earshot Easter laughter (*risus paschalis*). The comic ending is God's end in sight. Comedy not only has, but *reveals*, a teleology.

The mode was perhaps understood in this way by Dante, as a shape in and beyond time—as *commedia*. Medieval definitions of comedy tended to be strongly end-oriented: according to Uguccione da Pisa's *Magna Derivationes* (*c.*1200), tragedy ends badly, comedy ends well. A facetiously compressed summary of Dante's *Commedia* (1308–21) might be: 'a journey from "Well, I'll be damned!" to "Good God!"' The philosopher Giorgio Agamben suggests that Christ's death liberates man from tragedy and makes comedy possible: *'tragedy appears as the guilt of the just,'* he suggests, *'comedy as the justification of the guilty.'* Not *Mea Culpa*, then, but the *felix culpa*. To put things this way, though, is to occlude the question of where the agency lies for this experience of conversion. The comedy is not merely a divine one because Man has his own role to play, and the comic instinct has often been imagined as a free yet fluctuating will in a testing universe. Eugenio Montale wrote that 'when a man is besieged by the things around him…he can do nothing but engage in dialogue with them, maybe in an attempt to exorcise them. At this stage, there is born the comic style which achieved its greatest triumph in Dante's *Commedia.'* This emphasis on style brings out another meaning of *commedia* as understood and shaped by Dante: a hybrid, intermediate form of expression, a mixture of different styles and allegiances (high and low, literary and vernacular, religious and secular). In this sense, the poet's comic style practises the mediation its content preaches: a conversation between man's highest aspirations and 'the things around him' is conducted through the dialogics of the *Commedia*'s formal daring.

Many of comedy's endgames have been played on the edge of sacred ground. Samuel Taylor Coleridge's jottings for a lecture topic included the following idea: 'When we contemplate a finite in reference to an infinite, consciously or unconsciously, *humour*'. Humour, he explains, signifies 'Acknowledgement of the hollowness and farce of the world, and its disproportion to the godlike within us'. One route to the godlike is to resituate your pain in relation to eternity, to step back from pain as though you were seeing yourself as God might see you. In Herman Hesse's *Steppenwolf* (1929), it is remarked that seriousness consists in putting too high a value on time: 'In eternity, however, there is no time, you see. Eternity is a mere moment, just long enough for a joke.' A great appreciator and maker of such jokes is Emily Dickinson, who once confessed to a friend that, since he had gone away, 'We don't have many jokes, though, now, it is pretty much all sobriety; and we do not have much poetry, father having made up his mind that it's pretty much all real life.' Like a joke, a poem may aim to get beyond real life. But both forms need to begin from it, to weigh up the infinite *in reference to* the finite. Dickinson acknowledged that she sang off charnel steps, and the music of her songs carries an oddball comic lilt: 'I measure every Grief I meet | With narrow, probing Eyes— | I wonder if It weighs like Mine— | Or has an Easier size.' It sounds as if a curious look at the grief of others might allow you to transcend your own. The tone is neither pitiless nor pathetic: grief can sometimes feel interminable, but the ability to measure it suggests that there may be an end in sight.

Dickinson's writing often builds towards an end which is whimsical yet also hard-edged:

> It's easy to invent a Life—
> God does it—every Day—
> Creation—but the Gambol
> Of His Authority—
>
> It's easy to efface it—
> The thrifty Deity
> Could scarce afford Eternity
> To Spontaneity—
>
> The Perished Patterns murmur—
> But His Perturbless Plan
> Proceed—inserting Here—A Sun—
> There—leaving out a Man—

The poem doesn't only imagine a gambolling yet thrifty god, one who can make it, take it, *and* leave it; it also tries to cultivate a little of the Maker's attitude as the writing's own perturbless plan takes shape. Søren Kierkegaard provides the most sustained account of the relation between comical and Christian imaginings, and offers one way of entertaining this kind of gnomic wit. For him, the comic is an awareness of a contradiction—man's sense of himself, for example, as body and soul, or as temporal and eternal—and the Christian faith is built on a series of contradictions (the lowest as the highest; the meek inheriting the earth; the saviour on the donkey; and the Incarnation itself, the divine being in human form). 'The religious person,' from this perspective, 'is one who has discovered the comic on the greatest scale.' Dickinson's poem is bent on such discovery. The final two lines initially sound droll enough—something gained here, something lost there—but they also punningly hint at the Incarnation and the Passion, for God inserted here his Son *as* a Man and then oversaw the leaving out of that Man via his leave-taking on the cross. That end was not quite The End. The dash which closes this and so many other poems by Dickinson might stand as a figure for one particular kind of comic endgame: it marks the moment at which 'Perished' could also be read as 'Proceed'.

So comedy may be a road to redemption. That said, the comic imagining has frequently offered itself as salve rather than salvation. The gospel according to comedy needn't always be on the side of the angels (recall James Joyce's take on one particular resurrection: 'Come forth Lazarus, and he came fifth'). Franz Kafka's jokes come not from an anticipation of order, but from a feeling for mistimed arrival or superfluous conclusion. The Messiah, he said, would come only when he was no longer needed, not on the Last Day but on the day after that. He suggested to Max Brod that he sometimes saw the world as one of God's bad moods. Brod asked, 'So there would be hope outside our world?' 'Plenty of hope,' Kafka said, smiling, 'for God—no end of hope—only not for us.' It's hard to read that smile, but pondering it can help us to consider the ways in which some comedies take their energies from whatever it is that people think they *cannot* escape. Joseph K. notes that one could certainly regard his situation as 'a joke', and the first paragraph of *The Trial* (1925) ends like this: 'if this was a comedy he would insist on playing it to the end'. But maybe he plays along too readily, is so drawn to a need for an end somewhere (comedy must have one, apparently) that he abnegates his responsibility to shape that end. Brod recalled how Kafka laughed so much when reading the first chapter of *The Trial* to his friends that he couldn't go on. Again, it's not easy to tell what that laughter portends, but one source of hilarity may be that K.'s being such a stickler and searcher for the rules is a founding condition of his predicament. Witness a later exchange: '"But it's all nonsense." "What's nonsense?" asked K. "Why do you insist on asking?" said the corn-merchant, irritably.' It seems that K.'s drive for exegesis is a category error; he's trying to detect and decipher parables when he should be attending to something else altogether.

Not that we're any the wiser than K. Comedy often reminds us that we too are looking for meanings, motives, and ends in a constantly confusing world. Woody Allen—himself a grateful, gleeful reader of Kafka ('One day, for no apparent reason, F. broke his diet')—begins *Love and Death* (1975) by bemoaning the fact that he is to be executed for a crime he never committed: 'Of course, isn't all mankind in the same boat? Isn't all mankind ultimately executed for a crime it never committed?' One way of handling this text of the 'ultimate' is to turn it into a pretext for other considerations. Take this unholy trinity from across Woody's career—a Yes, a No, and a Maybe: 'There is no question that there is an unseen world. The problem is, how far is it from midtown and how late is it open?'; 'Not only is there no God, but try getting a plumber on weekends'; 'I keep wondering if there is an afterlife, and if there is will they be able to break a twenty?'

The philosopher Alenka Zupančič has recently asked: 'Is not the very existence of comedy and of the comical telling us most clearly that man is never just a man, and that his finitude is corroded by a passion which is precisely not cut to the measure of man and of his finitude? ... *Not only are we not infinite, we are not even finite.*' Yes, things may well be that bad, and these jokes seem to know it. Whether there's an afterlife or not, you can't give up on your major or minor passions; heaven promises much, but in a comic universe man will always need to conceive the heavenly in his own image.

In his playlet, 'Death Knocks' (1968), Woody pays playful tribute to Ingmar Bergman's *The Seventh Seal* (1957) by bringing the Grim Reaper down to earth: '(*He huffs audibly and then trips over the windowsill and falls into the room.*) DEATH (*for it is no one else*): Jesus Christ. I nearly broke my neck.' It is fitting that Christ should be on Death's mind, for the sketch is a parody of the Incarnation. This is the flip side of the comedy of looking down on ourselves from an infinite height; here we see a Timeless Truth entering and getting tangled up in time. Death waits for no man, but here he'll need to get his breath back before continuing. *Love and Death* draws to a close with the comment: 'The key is, to not think of death as an end, but think of it more of a very effective way of cutting down on your expenses.' Many comedies end with a similar imperative. It feels as though something is over, but don't *think* of it as an end. Think of an end point as a standpoint. Or, better, think that closure might be reconceived as adventure.

## Married to comedy

There are other consummations devoutly to be wished, of course, and the comic imagination has long been drawn to a different endgame: marriage. Shakespearean comedy makes the most of it. Happy endings abound, 'All's well that ends well,' and 'Jack shall have Jill, | Nought shall go ill,' as Puck jauntily puts it in *A Midsummer Night's Dream*. Yet this line needs to be heard alongside another from *Love's Labour's Lost*: 'Our wooing doth not end like an old play: | Jack hath not Jill,' Biron observes. Ferdinand replies: 'Come, sir, it wants a twelvemonth and a day, | And then 'twill end.' Biron isn't satisfied: 'That's too long for a play.' The implication is that comic endings demand a contrivance from the writer, and a knowing connivance with the audience. Eric Bentley suggested that comedies have to end fast, otherwise they may turn bad, so 'Happy endings are always ironical.' Possibly, although the irony does not necessarily give up on happiness, but rather asks us to consider what it is we and others seem to want from happiness. The ending of *Measure for Measure* (*c*.1603–4) pushes things to the limit by getting audiences to think about the suitability of marriage as a symbolic shorthand for comedy's happy-ever-afters. When Mariana enquires of the Duke, 'my most gracious lord, | I hope you will not mock me with a husband,' she is voicing her fear that she will lose her heart's desire, but the line also glances towards another possibility, for many would consider it a fate worse than death to be married to Angelo. The Duke's final words to Mariana as he marries the couple off ('Joy to you, Mariana') are uttered moments after Angelo himself has admitted: 'I crave death more willingly than mercy.'

*Measure for Measure* provides something other than comic business as usual, but its latent ironies are a vital part of comedy's bequest: the mode's endings are not just wish fulfilments, but provocations to further thought about the nature of the wishes themselves. Indeed, what is funny in many comedies *is* the happy ending. In Dickens's *Pickwick Papers* (1836–7), news of one marriage is received thus: '"Married!" exclaimed Pott, with frightful vehemence. He stopped, smiled darkly, and added, in a low, vindictive tone: "It serves him right!"' The final shot of Keaton's miniature masterpiece, *Sherlock Jr* (1924), is less dark, but it's not exactly light. It arrives just moments after Sherlock has landed the girl of his dreams by following the cues of the drawing-room comedy he's watching from the cinema's projection room (see Figure 17).

The final image on the movie screen he is watching presents the happy-ever-after he's been chasing (domestic bliss, wife, and two children), but he responds in bemusement, scratching his head, as if to say 'Is *this* what I wanted?' Keaton is also looking out at us too from behind the screen and behind his character: 'And you? What did *you* want?' George Bernard Shaw suggested that there are two tragedies in life: 'One is to lose your heart's desire. The other is to gain it.' Comic endings often sense the truth of this and so try to make room for a possibility beyond these tragedies by keeping other desires in play.

**17. Buster Keaton, *Sherlock Jr* (1924)**
**(To view This: http://youtu_be/d4LRyPOuaLM)**

Shaw's own difficulties with the ending of *Pygmalion* (1912)
concentrate and further this central question about closure and
comedy: what, precisely, does satisfaction mean? Is it a destination
or a side effect? In Ovid, Pygmalion marries Galatea after having
carved her out of ivory, but in the denouement of Shaw's drama
Eliza refuses to play along with Higgins and sweeps out with the
line: 'What you are to do without me I cannot imagine.' Shaw wrote
a prose sequel to the play questioning the assumption made by
many that she would return, and mocked those still in thrall to the
'stock of "happy endings" to misfit all stories'. Even the original
censor's report claimed that 'in the end she consents to come back',
and the later film version and the Broadway musical *My Fair Lady*
(1956) both played the final scene this way. Shaw's alternative
endings provide a more nuanced understanding of what his
comedy sets in motion. In the 1920 Aldwych Theatre version,
Higgins exclaims 'Galatea!' as he watches Eliza depart. In a letter

to the actress, the playwright glossed the word: '(meaning that the statue has come to life at last)…Thus he gets the last word; and you get it too.' The last word acknowledges that Eliza's coming to life is not a coming home to settle down. In Shaw's alternative film ending, Higgins is asked if anything is wrong: 'No: nothing wrong. A happy ending. A happy beginning.'

Here and elsewhere, comedy is conceived not as an end in itself, but as a means to other ends. The mode offers us an understanding of happiness as an intimation of unfinished business. The critic T. G. A. Nelson observes 'two contradictory, yet equally fundamental, tendencies of comedy, the impulse to laughter and the movement towards harmony' and sees these two tendencies in action most clearly in 'a tension between the forward movement of the plot, which is usually toward marriage, and the backward pull of the dialogue, which ridicules it'. This is helpful, but many comedies find ways of allowing both these tendencies to coalesce in one ending. The final moment of *Pygmalion* contains harmony *and* laughter: 'HIGGINS: She's going to marry Freddy! Ha ha! Freddy! Freddy!! Ha ha ha ha ha ha!!!!! [*He roars the laughter as the play ends.*]' Similarly in Shaw's *Man and Superman* (1903), which closes as Violet calls Jack Tanner a brute for casting aspersions on marriage. 'ANN: Never mind her, dear. Go on talking. TANNER: Talking! [*Universal laughter*]' Laughter at a moment like this is an attempt to laugh off the very ideal of 'harmony'. The ideal has been seen through and found wanting—from which it does not necessarily follow that the ideal is wanted any less.

Towards the end of *Middlemarch* (1871–2), George Eliot reminded readers that 'Marriage, which has been the bourne of so many narratives, is still a great beginning, as it was to Adam and Eve, who kept their honeymoon in Eden, but had their first little one among the thorns and thistles of the wilderness.' From *The Lady Eve* (1941) to *Adam's Rib* (1949) and beyond, the films that Stanley Cavell has termed Hollywood's 'comedies of remarriage' provide some of the richest, most radiant enquiries into the nature of bournes as new beginnings. Many of these films start outside Eden, where it seems that although paradise has been lost, the couple are still within calling distance. The question is not 'Will they get married?' but rather 'Will they stay divorced?' As Walter says to his ex-wife Hildy in *His Girl Friday* (1940), 'There's something between us that no divorce can come between.' Cavell notes that, if marriage was meant to be the joining of the sexual and the social, then it has turned out to be a disappointment, perhaps on account of its impotence to domesticate sexuality without discouraging it. What these films search for is another version of comedy's long-standing rhythm of rebirth from death by moving towards a mutual willingness for remarriage: 'we discover, or recover, romance within the arena of marriage itself…turn marriage itself into romance…into the capacity to notice one another, to remember beginning, to remember that you are strangers'.

To remember beginning: this is the cherished knowledge of many comic endings, and it makes comedy something more like a hope than a promise. At the end of *The Philadelphia Story* (1940), Dexter asks Tracy to remarry him. She replies, 'Dexter, are you sure?' 'Not in the least, but I'll risk it, will you?' At moments like this, comedy aims for something more complex than reassurance. The genre breathes audacity, peril, improvisation. If it yearns for the stability and security that marriages and endings can provide, it is also in league with the hope that the risks of romance will never end. In the final scene of *The Awful Truth* (1937), Jerry puts it well when he confesses to Lucy: 'You're still the same, only I've been a fool. Well, I'm not now. So long as I'm different don't you think that things could be the same again, only a little different?' Perhaps they could, perhaps they will. What we are offered here is not plenitude, but prolepsis. Not quite happiness exactly, but the imagination of happiness.

Howard Hawks archly said of *Bringing Up Baby* (1938) that he had provided 'a rather happy ending'. In the final scene Susan speaks for

**18. Howard Hawks, _Bringing Up Baby_ (1938)**
(To view This: http://youtu_be/BibrhVUSAvo)

Hawks's adjective when she assures David: 'Everything's going to be all right.' David, though, speaks for the adverb when he replies: 'Every time you say that, something happens.' (See Figure 18.)

Adam and Eve almost fall again, but not quite. Modern comedy has increasingly come to end not when everything is all right, but when it's _going to be_ all right (maybe). It gestures towards a future that cannot be known, saying not so much that 'They both lived happily ever after,' but that 'They lived'—nothing less than this, and the hopes which go along with it. As Sir Peter Teazle says to the young lovers at the end of Sheridan's _The School for Scandal_: 'may you live as happily together as Lady Teazle and I—intend to do.' In this incarnation, the comic ending is the art of the penultimate, which is why its last moments are so often charged with the feeling that the conversation has slightly stalled even as we sense a willingness to continue that conversation beyond the end of the film. The wonderful exchange of words and looks that closes Woody Allen's *Manhattan* (1979) captures this spirit. Billy Wilder also nails it in *The Apartment* (1960)—Bud: 'Did you hear what I said, Miss Kubelick? I absolutely adore you.' Fran (*smiling*): 'Shut up and deal!' *Some Like it Hot* (1959) is even better: 'Osgood, I'm gonna level with you. We can't get married at all.' 'Why not?' 'I'm a man.' 'Well, nobody's perfect.'

Comedy, if it's committed to anything, is committed to this lack of perfection, both to what it costs and what it brings, and the genre's most moving endgames continue to return to it. In the final moments of *Eternal Sunshine of the Spotless Mind* (2004), Clementine and Joel face up to the difficulty of beginning things again:

> CLEMENTINE: I'm not a concept, Joel. I'm just a fucked-up girl who's looking for my own peace of mind. I'm not perfect.
> JOEL: I can't see anything that I don't like about you right now.
> CLEMENTINE: But you will. You will. You will think of things. And I'll get bored with you and feel trapped because that's what happens with me.
> JOEL: Okay.
> CLEMENTINE [laughing through tears]: Okay...Okay.
> JOEL [laughing, crying]: Okay.
> Charlie Kaufman, *Eternal Sunshine of the Spotless Mind*

Joel's 'Okay' is something between a concession and an objection. Clementine's are surprised, incredulous, relieved. Their shared laughter is an old song and a new start. As they laugh, Beck's version of 'Everybody's Got to Learn Sometime' cradles the film to a close. This Sometime is the time of the comic ending. It includes the feeling that it's hard to begin afresh, but it also takes its bearings from the song's opening words: 'Change your heart. Look around you.' This is one of the gifts of comedy: its willingness to take in—and to take on—something different. As Lorrie Moore puts it in *A Gate at the Stairs* (2009): 'That's how you knew it was a comedy. The end of comedy was the beginning of all else.'

# Publisher's Acknowledgements

We are grateful for permission to include the following copyright material in this book.

Elizabeth Bishop: lines from 'The Wit' from *Complete Poems 1911–1979* with an introduction by Tom Paulin (Chatto & Windus, 2004), copyright © 1979, 1983, by Alice Helen Methfessel, reprinted by permission of Farrar, Straus & Giroux, LLC.

Peter Cook and Dudley Moore: extract from 'This bloke came up to me' from *Derek and Clive: Live* (Island Masters Records, 1989), reprinted by permission of David Higham Associates for the estates of the authors.

Talking Heads: extracts from '(Nothing But) Flowers', words and music by David Byrne, Jerry Harrison, Chris Frantz, Tina Weymouth, and Yves N'Jock, copyright © 1988 Index Music, Inc. (ASCAP); reprinted by permission of Warner Chappell Music Ltd. All rights administered by WB Music Corp.

We have made every effort to trace and contact all copyright holders before publication. If notified, the publisher will be pleased to rectify any errors or omissions at the earliest opportunity.

# References

Quotations from Shakespeare's plays are from the *Complete Works*, edited by Jonathan Bate and Eric Rasmussen (Basingstoke: Macmillan, 2007). All quotations from the Bible are from the King James Version. Space does not allow for the citation of every work quoted in the main text, so I have tended to give references just for secondary critical material. For authors writing in languages other than English, I have used the following translations: Euripides (J. Michael Walton); Aristophanes (David Barrett and Alan Sommerstein); Menander (Norma Miller); Terence (Peter Browne); Plautus (E. F. Watling and Erich Segal); Horace and Juvenal (Niall Rudd); Machiavelli (David Sices and James Atkinson); Erasmus (Clarence Miller); Rabelais and Montaigne (M. A. Screech); Cervantes (Edith Grossman); Molière (Donald Frame); Goldoni (Lee Hall); Beaumarchais (David Coward); Voltaire (Theo Cuff); Flaubert (A. J. Krailsheimer); Pushkin (Charles Johnson); Gogol (Richard Pevear and Larissa Volokhonsky); Chekhov (Michael Frayn); Kafka (Max Brod); Svevo (William Weaver); Ionesco (Donald Allen, Derek Prouse, and Donald Watson).

## Curtain raiser

Plato, *Philebus*, tr. Benjamin Jowett, *Three Dialogues: Protagoras, Philebus, and Gorgias* (New York: Cosimo, 2010), p. 97.

Saul Steinberg, quoted in Harry Levin, *Playboys and Killjoys: An Essay on the Theory and Practice of Comedy* (New York: Oxford University Press, 1987), p. 191.

Buster Keaton, quoted in Edward McPherson, *Buster Keaton: Tempest in a Flat Hat* (London: Faber and Faber, 2004), p. xiv.

Theodor Lipps, quoted in Sigmund Freud, *The Joke and Its Relation to the Unconscious*, tr. Joyce Crick (London: Penguin, 2002), p. 7.

Max Eastman, *Enjoyment of Laughter* (1936; repr. New Brunswick, NJ: Transaction, 2009), p. 41.

Ludwig Wittgenstein, in Norman Malcolm, *Ludwig Wittgenstein: A Memoir* (Oxford: Oxford University Press, 1958), p. 29.

Paolo Virno, *Multitude: Between Innovation and Negation* (Los Angeles: Semiotext(e), 2008), pp. 103–4.

Theodor W. Adorno and Max Horkheimer, *Dialectic of Enlightenment*, tr. Edmund Jephcott (London: Verso, 1997), p. 140.

Sigmund Freud, *The Joke and Its Relation to the Unconscious*, tr. Joyce Crick (London: Penguin, 2002), p. 149.

Ronald de Sousa, *The Rationality of Emotion* (Cambridge, MA: MIT Press, 1987), p. 282.

## Chapter 1 In the beginning...

Kenneth Dover, *Aristophanic Comedy* (Berkeley: University of California Press, 1972), p. 219.

*Tractatus Coislinianus*, in *The Birth of Comedy: Texts, Documents, and Art from Athenian Comic Competitions, 486–280*, ed. Jeffrey Rusten, tr. Jeffrey Henderson et al. (Baltimore: Johns Hopkins University Press, 2011), p. 732.

Antiphanes, *Poesis*, in *The Birth of Comedy: Texts, Documents, and Art from Athenian Comic Competitions, 486–280*, ed. Jeffrey Rusten, tr. Jeffrey Henderson et al. (Baltimore: Johns Hopkins University Press, 2011), p. 507.

Mary Douglas, *Implicit Meanings: Selected Essays in Anthropology*, 2nd edn (New York and London: Routledge, 1999), pp. 150, 155, 160.

Maurice Blanchot, *Friendship* (1971), tr. Elizabeth Rottenberg (Stanford: Stanford University Press, 1997), p. 181.

Northrop Frye, *Anatomy of Criticism: Four Essays* (Princeton, NJ: Princeton University Press, 1957), pp. 182–3.

Phillip Stubbes, quoted in C. L. Barber, *Shakespeare's Festive Comedy: A Study of Dramatic Form and its Relation to Social Custom* (Princeton, NJ: Princeton University Press, 1972), pp. 22, 28.

Mikhail Bakhtin, *Rabelais and His World* (1965), tr. Helene Iswolsky (Blooomington, IN: Indiana University Press, 1984), pp. 149, 21.

Randall Jarrell, *A Sad Heart at the Supermarket: Essays & Fables* (London: Etre & Spottiswode, 1965), p. 19.

Charles Baudelaire, quoted in André Breton, *Anthology of Black Humor* (San Fransisco, CA: City Light Books, 1997), p. 205.

Press report on Dublin riots, *Freeman's Journal*, 31 January 1907, p. 7.

Bruce Robinson, quoted in Kevin Jackson, *Withnail and I* (London: British Film Institute, 2004), p. 27.

Joris-Karl Huysmans, quoted in Walter Redfern, *French Laughter: Literary Humour from Diderot to Tournier* (Oxford: Oxford University Press, 2008), p. 63.

## Chapter 2 Getting physical

René Descartes, *The Passions of The Soul* (1649), tr. Stephen H. Voss (Indianapolis, IN: Hackett, 1989), p. 84.

Charles Bell, *The Anatomy and Philosophy of Expression as Connected to the Fine Arts* (London: George Bell, 1888), p. 31.

Charles Darwin, *The Expression of the Emotions in Man and Animals* (Oxford: Oxford University Press, 1998), p. 206.

Arthur Koestler, *The Act of Creation* (London: Hutchinson, 1964), p. 63.

Max Beerbohm, *And Even Now* (London: Heinemann, 1920), p. 307.

Jean Paul Richter, quoted by M. S. Silk in *Aristophanes and the Definition of Comedy* (Oxford: Oxford University Press, 2000), p. 95.

Mikhail Bakhtin, *Rabelais and His World* (1965), tr. Helene Iswolsky (Blooomington, IN: Indiana University Press, 1984), pp. 316–7, 325.

C. S. Lewis, *Miracles: A Preliminary Study* (1947), quoted in *A Year With C. S. Lewis* (London: HarperCollins, 2003), p. 79.

Jorge Luis Borges, *Labyrinths: Selected Stories and Other Writings*, ed. Donald A. Yates and James E. Irby (London: Penguin, 2000), p. 250.

William Makepeace Thackeray, 'On Charity and Humor', repr. in *English Humorists of The Eighteenth Century* (London: Macmillan, 1910), p. 275.

Byron, *Byron's Letters and Journals*, ed. Leslie A. Marshand, 11 vols. (London: John Murray, 1973–81), iii. 239.

Eugene Ionesco, quoted in J. L. Styan, *Drama, Stage and Audience* (Cambridge: Cambridge University Press, 1975), p. 84.

Henri Bergson, *Laughter* (1900), in *Comedy*, ed. Wylie Sypher (Baltimore: Johns Hopkins University Press, 1980), p. 79.

Wyndham Lewis, *The Complete Wild Body* (Santa Barbara: Black Sparrow Press, 1982), pp. 158–9.

Alain Robbe-Grillet, *Why I Love Roland Barthes* (Cambridge: Polity, 2011), p. 13.

Philip Roth, interview with Mark Lawson, Radio 4, *Front Row* (27 June 2011).

## Chapter 3 In and out of character

Henri Bergson, *Laughter* (1900), in *Comedy*, ed. Wylie Sypher (Baltimore: Johns Hopkins University Press, 1980), pp. 156, 84, 82.

George Meredith, *An Essay on Comedy and The Uses of The Comic Spirit* (1877), in *Comedy*, ed. Wylie Sypher (Baltimore: Johns Hopkins University Press, 1980), p. 47.

G. K. Chesterton, entry on 'Humour' for the *Encyclopedia Britannica* (1938).

Ralph Waldo Emerson, 'The Comic' in *Letters and Social Aims* (London: Chatto & Windus, 1876), p. 137.

Annibale Carracci, quoted in *English Caricature: 1620 to the Present* (London: Victoria and Albert Museum, 1984), p. 11.

William Hazlitt, 'Wit and Humour', in *Lectures on the English Comic Writers*, in *The Complete Works of William Hazlitt*, ed. P. P. Howe, 21 vols. (London: Dent, 1930–34), vi. 140, 138.

Samuel Johnson, Rambler no. 75 (1750), in *The Yale Edition of the Works of Samuel Johnson*, Volume IV, ed. Walter Jackson Bate and Albrecht B. Strauss (New Haven: Yale University Press, 1969), ii. 33.

Lord George Gordon Byron, *The Complete Miscellaneous Prose*, ed. Andrew Nicholson (Oxford: Oxford University Press, 1991), pp. 192–3.

Oscar Wilde, *Epigrams of Oscar Wilde* (Ware: Wordsworth Editions, 2007), p. 56.

Groucho Marx, quoted in Alan Dale, *Comedy is a Man in Trouble: Slapstick in the American Movies* (Minneapolis: University of Minnesota Press, 2000), p. 159.

George S. Kaufman, quoted in Stefan Kanfer, *Groucho: The Life and Times of Julius Henry Marx* (New York: Knopf Doubleday, 2001), p. 93.

Charles Baudelaire, *Selected Writings on Art and Literature*, tr. P. E. Charvet (London: Penguin, 2006), p. 160.

## Chapter 4 Plotting mischief

Cicero, *On The Orator*, Book II, chapter 63, quoted in John Morreall, ed. *The Philosophy of Laughter and Humor* (New York: State University of New York Press, 1987), p. 18.

Immanuel Kant, *Critique of the Power of Judgement* (1790), tr. Paul Guyer and Eric Matthews (Cambridge: Cambridge University Press, 2001), p. 209.

A. P. Herbert, *The English Laugh* (Oxford: Oxford University Press, 1950), p. 6.

Daniel C. Dennett, Matthew M. Hurley, and Reginald B. Adams, Jr., *Inside Jokes: Using Humor to Reverse-Engineer the Mind* (Cambridge, MA: MIT Press, 2011), p. 265.

August Wilhelm von Schlegel, *Lectures on Dramatic Art and Literature* (1808), tr. John Black, quoted in Paul Lauter, ed., *Theories of Comedy* (New York: Anchor Books, 1964), p. 338.

Susanne Langer, 'The Comic Rhythm', in *Feeling and Form* (London: Routledge and Kegan Paul, 1953), p. 333.

Louis Pasteur and James Joyce, both quoted in Lewis Hyde, *Trickster Makes the World: How Disruptive Imagination Creates Culture* (London: Canongate, 1998), pp. 140–41.

E. M. Forster, *Aspects of the Novel* (1927), ed. Oliver Stallybrass (London: Penguin, 1990), p. 43.

Ludwig Wittgenstein, *Culture and Value*, tr. Peter Winch, ed. G. H. Von Wright (Chicago: University of Chicago Press, 1984), 7e.

Eugene Ionesco, *Time* (New York, 12 December 1960); interview in *L'Express* (28 January 1960).

Deleted line from *Groundhog Day*, cited in Ryan Gilbey, *Groundhog Day* (London: British Film Institute, 2004), p. 21.

## Chapter 5 Underdogs

Plato, *The Republic*, tr. Benjamin Jowett, (1894; repr. New York: Cosimo, 2008), p. 264.

Friedrich Nietzsche, *The Gay Science*, tr. Walter Kaufmann (New York: Vintage, 1974), pp. 316–17.

Aristotle and Donatus, quoted in Paul Lauter, ed., *Theories of Comedy* (New York: Anchor Books, 1964), pp. 13, 29.

Dario Fo, *The Tricks of The Trade* (New York: Methuen, 1991), p. 172.

Enid Welsford, *The Fool: His Social and Literary History* (New York: Anchor, 1961), p. 324.

References

Mozart, *Seven Mozart Librettos*, tr. J. D. McClatchy (New York: Norton, 2011), p. 463.

Grimaldi review, cited in Andrew McConnell Stott, *The Pantomime Life of Joseph Grimaldi* (London: Canongate, 2009), pp. 119, 200.

Fernando Pessoa, *A Centenary Pessoa*, ed. Eugenio Lisboa and L. C. Taylor (Manchester: Carcanet, 1997), p. 275.

Sandor Ferenczi, 'Laughter' (1913), in *Final Contributions to the Problems and Methods of Psychoanalysis* (London: Karnac, 2002), p. 178.

Federico Fellini, *A Journey into the Shadow: Reflections and Original Drawings on the Making of the Clowns*, ed. Adriano Apra (accompanying booklet with DVD; Raro Video, 2011), pp. 25, 13.

Stephen Sondheim, interview with Mel Gussow in the *New York Times* (11 March 2003).

Eddie Izzard, interview in *The Independent* (23rd May 2004).

Bill Hicks, BBC2 (1992)—see: http://youtu.be/aKXZ2EzW7gw

Stewart Lee, *How I Escaped My Certain Fate: The Life and Deaths of a Stand-Up Comedian* (London: Faber and Faber, 2010), pp. 200, 99, 87, 220.

David Baddiel and Ricky Gervais, *The Office at 10*, see: http://www.bbc.co.uk/comedy/theoffice/videos/index.shtml

## Chapter 6 Taking liberties

Charles Baudelaire, *Selected Writings on Art and Literature*, tr. P. E. Charvet (London: Penguin, 2006), p. 143.

Norbert Elias, 'Essay on Laughter' (unpublished manuscript), quoted in Anca Parvulescu, *Laughter: Notes on A Passion* (Massachusetts, CA: MIT Press, 2010), p. 141.

V. S. Ramachandran and Sandra Blakeslee, *Phantoms in the Brain* (London: Harper Perennial, 2005), pp. 199–211.

Robert Provine, *Laughter: A Scientific Investigation* (London: Faber and Faber, 2000), pp. 75–128.

Aristotle, *Nicomachean Ethics*, Book IV, ch. 8, Plato, and Descartes, all quoted in John Morreall, ed. *The Philosophy of Laughter and Humor* (New York: State University of New York Press, 1987), pp. 15, 12, 24.

W. H. Auden, 'Notes on the Comic' in *The Dyer's Hand* (New York: Vintage, 1968), p. 383.

Walter Benjamin, *Selected Writings: Part 2, 1931–34*, ed. Michael William Jennings and Howard Eiland (Cambridge, MA: Harvard University Press, 2005), p. 448.

Dryden, 'A Discourse on Satire', in *The Poetical Works*, ed. Joseph Warton et al, 4 vols. (London: Cadell and Davies, 1811) iv. 247.

Thomas Hobbes, *Human Nature* (1651), quoted in John Morreall, ed. *The Philosophy of Laughter and Humor* (New York: State University of New York Press, 1987), p. 20.

Lord Shaftesbury, *Characteristics of Men, Manners, Opinions, Times* (1711), ed. L. Klein (Cambridge: Cambridge University Press, 1999), p. 31.

Alexander Pope, *The Correspondence of Alexander Pope*, ed. George Sherburn, 5 vols. (Oxford: Clarendeon Press, 1956), i. 211–12.

Adam Phillips, *On Kissing, Tickling, and Being Bored* (London: Faber and Faber, 1994), p. 2.

Kenneth Burke, *The Philosophy of Literary Form: Studies in Symbolic Action*, 3rd edn (Berkeley, CA: University of California Press, 1973), pp. 320–1.

John Cage, quoted in *Happenings and Other Acts*, ed. Mariellen R. Sandford (London: Routledge, 1995), p. 66.

Charles Lamb, quoted in *The Idea of Comedy: Essays in Prose and Verse*, ed. W. K. Wimsatt (Englewood Cliffs, NJ: Prentice-Hall, 1969), pp. 224–5.

Jane Austen, letter to Fanny Knight (March 1817), quoted in David Nokes, *Jane Austen: A Life* (Berkeley, CA: University of California Press, 1997), p. 520.

Theodore Martin, 'William Edmonstoune Aytoun', *Blackwood's Magazine*, 103 (April 1868), p. 444.

Max Beerbohm, in N. John Hall, *Caricatures* (New Haven: Yale University Press, 1997), p. 16; *A Christmas Garland*, ed. N. John Hall (New Haven: Yale University Press, 1993), p. xi.

Evelyn Waugh, *Essays, Articles and Reviews*, ed. Donat Gallagher (London: Methuen, 1983), p. 304.

Gore Vidal, 'The Satiric World of Evelyn Waugh', *New York Times* (7 January 1962).

George Orwell, in the *Leader* (28th July 1945).

Geoffrey Grigson, ed., *The Oxford Book of Satirical Verse* (Oxford: Oxford University Press, 1980), p. v.

## Chapter 7 Beyond a joke

Flann O'Brien, cited in Colm Tóibín, 'Flann O'Brien's Lies', *London Review of Books* (5 January 2012).

Friedrich Nietzsche, *Philosophical Writings*, ed. Reinhold Grimm and Caroline Molina y Vedia (New York: Continuum, 1997), p. 241.

Sigmund Freud, *The Joke and Its Relation to the Unconscious* (1905)
tr. Joyce Crick (London: Penguin, 2002), pp. 98–9; 'Humour'
(1928), in *The Penguin Freud Reader*, ed. Adam Phillips (London:
Penguin, 2006), pp. 561, 566.

Horace Walpole, quoted in *The Idea of Comedy: Essays in Prose and
Verse*, ed. W. K. Wimsatt (Englewood Cliffs, NJ: Prentice-Hall,
1969), p. 193.

Plato, *Symposium*, in *The Idea of Comedy*, ed. W. K. Wimsatt
(Englewood Cliffs, NJ: Prentice-Hall, 1969), p. 6.

Christopher Fry, 'Comedy', in *The Adelphi*, 27.1 (November 1950),
p. 28.

Aristophanes, on 'trugoidia', see M. S. Silk, *Aristophanes and the
Definition of Comedy* (Oxford: Oxford University Press, 2000),
pp. 42ff, 435.

Stephen Halliwell, *Greek Laughter: A Study of Cultural Psychology
from Homer to Early Christianity* (Cambridge: Cambridge
University Press, 2008), pp. 129–30.

Max Eastman, *The Sense of Humor* (London: Scribner, 1921), p. 11.

D. W. Winnicott, *Playing and Reality* (1971; repr. London: Routledge,
2005), p. 89.

André Breton, *Anthology of Black Humor* (San Fransisco, CA: City
Light Books, 1997), p. xix.

Arthur Schopenhauer, *The World as Will and Idea* (1844),
tr. R. B. Haldane and J. Kemp (London: Routledge and Kegan
Paul, 1907–9), p. 282.

Luigi Pirandello, *On Humor* (1920), tr. Antonio Illiano and Daniel P.
Testa (Chapel Hill, NC: University of North Carolina Press, 1977),
p. 118.

Nikolai Gogol, on the comic, cited by Donald Fanger, *The Creation of
Nikolai Gogol* (Cambridge, MA: Harvard University Press, 1979),
p. 125.

Anton Chekhov, on 'success', quoted in Ronald Hingley, *Chekhov*
(London: Allen and Unwin, 1950), p. 211.

Thomas Mann, *Altes und Neues* (Stockholm: Fischer, 1953), p. 501.

Samuel Beckett, on Endgame, quoted in *Beckett in The Theatre: Vol 1*,
ed. Dougald McMillan and Martha Fehsenfeld (London: John
Calder, 1988), p. 210.

Thomas Nagel, 'The Absurd', in *Mortal Questions* (Cambridge:
Cambridge University Press, 1979), p. 21.

Samuel Beckett, letter to Thomas MacGreevy, 9th September 1935
(Trinity College Dublin MS 10381).

Helmuth Plessner, *Laughing and Crying: A Study of The Limits of Human Behaviour*, tr. James Spencer Churchill and Marjorie Grene (Evanston: Northwestern University Press, 1970), pp. 79, 114.

## Chapter 8 Endgames

Michel de Montaigne, *The Complete Essays*, tr. M. A. Screech (London: Penguin, 1991), pp. 283, 340.

Sigmund Freud, 'Thoughts on Times of War and Death' (1915), in *Collected Papers* (London: Hogarth, 1925), iv. pp. 304–5.

Hallam Tennyson, *Alfred, Lord Tennyson: A Memoir by His Son*, 2 vols (London: Macmillan, 1897), i. 326.

Northrop Frye, 'The Argument of Comedy', in *English Institute Essays: 1948*, ed. D. A. Robertson (New York: Columbia University Press, 1949), pp. 66, 64.

Giorgio Agamben, 'Comedy', in *The End of the Poem*, tr. Daniel Heller-Roazen (Stanford, CA: Stanford University Press, 1999), p. 8.

Eugenio Montale, 'Finche l'assedio dura . . .' (1973), quoted in Eric Griffiths and Matthew Reynolds, ed., *Dante in English* (London: Penguin, 2005), p. lxxxv.

Samuel Taylor Coleridge, *Miscellaneous Criticism*, ed. Thomas Middleton Raysor (London: Constable, 1936), pp. 118, 119.

Emily Dickinson, *Letters of Emily Dickinson*, ed. Mabel Loomis Todd (Mineola, NY: Dover, 2003), p. 67.

Søren Kierkegaard, *Concluding Unscientific Postscript* to Philosophical Fragments, Volume 1, ed. and tr. Howard V. Hong and Edna H. Hong (Princeton: Princeton University Press, 1992), p. 462.

Franz Kafka, quoted in Michael Wood, *Franz Kafka* (London: Northcote, 2003), pp. 17, 13; Max Brod, *Kafka: A Biography*, tr. G. H. Roberts (London: Secker and Warburg, 1947), p. 139.

Woody Allen, *Complete Prose* (London: Picador, 1997), pp. 369, 15, 173, 8, 186.

Alenka Zupančič, *The Odd One In: On Comedy* (Cambridge, MA: MIT Press, 2008), pp. 49, 53.

Eric Bentley, *The Life of the Drama* (London: Methuen, 1969), p. 301.

T. G. A. Nelson, *Comedy: The Theory of Comedy in Literature, Drama, and Cinema* (Oxford: Oxford University Press, 1990), pp. 2, 46.

Stanley Cavell, *Pursuits of Happiness: The Hollywood Comedy of Remarriage* (Cambridge, MA: Harvard University Press, 1981), pp. 54, 186, 216.

Howard Hawks, quoted in Peter Bogdanovich, *Who The Devil Made It: Conversations with Legendary Film Directors* (New York: Knopf, 1997), pp. 305–6.

Comedy

# Further reading

## Anthologies of comic theory

J. Figueroa-Dorrego and C. Larkin-Galinanes, eds., *A Source Book of Literary and Philosophical Writings About Humour and Laughter* (London: Edwin Mellen Press, 2009).

Paul Lauter, ed., *Theories of Comedy* (New York: Anchor Books, 1964).

John Morreall, ed., *The Philosophy of Laughter and Humor* (New York: State University of New York Press, 1987).

W. K. Wimsatt, ed., *The Idea of Comedy: Essays in Prose and Verse* (Englewood Cliffs, NJ: Prentice-Hall, 1969).

## Introductions to comedy and its close relations

Richard Boston, *An Anatomy of Laughter* (London: Collins, 1974).

Maurice Charney, *Comedy High and Low: An Introduction to the Experience of Comedy* (Oxford: Oxford University Press, 1978).

Simon Critchley, *On Humour* (London: Routledge, 2002).

Simon Dentith, *Parody* (London: Routledge, 2000).

Dustin Griffin, *Satire: A Critical Reintroduction* (Lexington: University Press of Kentucky, 1994).

Hugh Haughton, ed., 'Introduction', *The Chatto Book of Nonsense Poetry* (London: Chatto and Windus, 1988).

Howard Jacobson, *Seriously Funny: From the Ridiculous to the Sublime* (London: Viking, 1997).

John Morreall, *Comic Relief: A Comprehensive Philosophy of Humor* (Oxford: Wiley-Blackwell, 2009).

T. G. A. Nelson, *Comedy: An Introduction* (Oxford: Oxford University Press, 1990).

D. J. Palmer, ed., *Comedy: Developments in Criticism* (Houndmills: Palgrave, 1992).

Andrew Stott, *Comedy* (New York: Routledge, 2005).

## More specialized studies

Michael Billig, *Laughter and Ridicule: Towards a Social Critique of Humour* (Nottingham, Sage, 2005).

Jan Bremmer and Herman Roodenburg, eds., *A Cultural History of Humour From Antiquity to The Present Day* (Cambridge: Polity, 1997).

Terry Castle, *Masquerade and Civilization: Carnivalesque in Eighteenth-Century English Culture and Fiction* (Stanford, CA: Stanford University Press, 1986).

Michael Cordner, Peter Holland and John Kerrigan, eds., *English Comedy* (Cambridge: Cambridge University Press, 1994).

Robert C. Elliott, *The Power of Satire: Magic, Ritual, Art* (Princeton, MA: Princeton University Press, 1960).

William Empson, 'Alice in Wonderland: The Child as Swain', in *Some Versions of Pastoral* (1935; repr. New York: New Directions, 1974).

William Empson, 'Wit in the *Essay on Criticism*', 'The Praise of Folly', and 'Fool in *Lear*', in *The Structure of Complex Words* (1951; repr. London: Penguin, 1995).

Roger B. Henkle, *Comedy and Culture: England 1820–1900* (Princeton, NJ: Princeton University Press, 1980).

Harry Levin, *Playboys and Killjoys: An Essay on the Theory and Practice of Comedy* (Oxford: Oxford University Press, 1987).

Michael North, *Machine-Age Comedy* (Oxford: Oxford University Press, 2009).

Claude Rawson, ed., *English Satire and the Satiric Tradition* (Oxford: Blackwell, 1984).

Claude Rawson, *Satire and Sentiment, 1660–1830: Stress Points in the English Augustan Tradition* (New Haven: Yale University Press, 2000).

Walter Redfern, *French Laughter: Literary Humour from Diderot to Tournier* (Oxford: Oxford University Press, 2008).

Susan Stewart, *Nonsense: Aspects of Intertextuality in Folklore and Literature* (Baltimore: Johns Hopkins University Press, 1979).

Stuart Tave, *The Amiable Humorist: A Study in the Comic Theory and Criticism of the Eighteenth and Early Nineteenth Centuries* (Chicago: Chicago University Press, 1967).

Richard Terry, *Mock-Heroic from Butler to Cowper: An English Genre and Discourse* (Aldershot: Ashgate, 2005).

## Classical perspectives

A. M. Bowie, *Aristophanes: Myth, Ritual and Comedy* (Cambridge: Cambridge University Press, 1996).

Francis MacDonald Cornford, *The Origin of Attic Comedy* (New York, Anchor, 1961).

Kenneth Dover, *Aristophanic Comedy* (Berkeley: University of California Press, 1972).

Stephen Halliwell, *Greek Laughter: A Study of Cultural Psychology from Homer to Early Christianity* (Cambridge: Cambridge University Press, 2008).

N. J. Lowe, *Comedy* (Cambridge: Cambridge University Press, 2008).

Maria Plaza, *The Function of Humour in Roman Verse Satire: Laughing and Lying* (Oxford: Oxford University Press, 2007).

Ralph M. Rosen, *Making Mockery: The Poetics of Ancient Satire* (Oxford: Oxford University Press, 2007).

M. S. Silk, *Aristophanes and The Definition of Comedy* (Oxford: Oxford University Press, 2000).

## Laughter

David Appelbaum, 'The Laugh' in *Voice* (New York: State University of New York, 1991).

Charles Baudelaire, 'On The Essence of Laughter', in *Selected Writings on Art and Literature*, tr. P. E. Charvet (London: Penguin, 2006).

James Beattie, *On Laughter and Ludicrous Composition*, 3rd edn (London: Dilly, 1779).

Max Beerbohm, 'Laughter', in *And Even Now* (London: Heinemann, 1920).

Henri Bergson, *Laughter* (1900), in *Comedy*, ed. Wylie Sypher (Baltimore: Johns Hopkins University Press, 1980).

Mikkel Borch-Jacobsen, 'The Laughter of Being', in *Bataille: A Critical Reader*, ed. Fred Botting and Scott Wilson (Oxford: Blackwell, 1998).

Brian Boyd, 'Laughter and Literature: A Play Theory of Humor', in *Philosophy and Literature*, 28 (2004), pp. 1–22.

Ronald de Sousa, 'When is it Wrong to Laugh?' in *The Rationality of Emotion* (Cambridge, MA: MIT Press, 1987).

Toby Garfitt, Edith McMorran and Jane Taylor, eds., *The Anatomy of Laughter* (London: Legenda, 2005).

Anca Parvulescu, *Laughter: Notes on A Passion* (Cambridge, MA: MIT Press, 2010).

Helmuth Plessner, *Laughing and Crying: A Study of the Limits of Human Behaviour*, tr. James Spencer Churchill and Majorie Grene (Evanston: Northwestern University Press, 1970).

Robert R. Provine, *Laughter: A Scientific Investigation* (London: Faber and Faber, 2000).

V. S. Ramachandran and Sandra Blakeslee, *Phantoms in the Brain* (London: Harper Perennial, 2005).

## Jokes

Jimmy Carr and Lucy Greeves, *The Naked Jape: Uncovering the Hidden World of Jokes* (London: Michael Joseph, 2006).

Ted Cohen, *Jokes: Philosophical Thoughts on Joking Matters* (Chicago: University of Chicago Press, 1999).

Mary Douglas, 'Jokes', in *Implicit Meanings: Selected Essays in Anthropology*, 2nd edn (New York and London: Routledge, 1999).

Jim Holt, *Stop Me If You've Heard This: A History and Philosophy of Jokes* (London: Profile, 2008).

Matthew M. Hurley, Daniel C. Dennett, and Reginald B. Adams, Jr., *Inside Jokes: Using Humor to Reverse-Engineer the Mind* (Cambridge, MA: MIT Press, 2011).

Christopher Ricks, 'The Irish Bull', in *Beckett's Dying Words* (Oxford: Clarendon Press, 1995).

Paolo Virno, 'Jokes and Innovative Action', in *Multitude: Between Innovation and Negation*, tr. Isabella Bertoletti, James Cascaito and Andrea Casson (Cambridge, MA: MIT Press, 2007).

## Play theory

Roger Caillois, tr. Meyer Barash, *Man, Play and Games* (Chicago, IL: University of Illionois Press, 2001).

Johan Huizinga, *Homo Ludens: A Study of the Play Element of Culture* (Boston: Beacon Press, 1950).

Mihai I Spariosu, *Dionysus Reborn: Play and The Aesthetic Dimension in Modern Philosophical and Scientific Discourse* (Ithaca & London: Cornell University Press, 1989).

Jean Piaget, *Play, Dreams and Imitation in Childhood*, tr. C. Gattegno and F. M. Hodgson (London: Routledge and Kegan Paul, 1951).

Brian Sutton-Smith, *The Ambiguity of Play* (Cambridge, MA: Harvard U. P., 2001).

D. W. Winnicott, *Playing and Reality* (1971; repr. London: Routledge, 2002).

## Drama

C. L. Barber, *Shakespeare's Festive Comedy: A Study of Dramatic Form and Its Relation to Social Custom* (Princeton, NJ: Princeton University Press, 1959).

Albert Bermel, *Farce: A History from Aristophanes to Woody Allen* (New York: Simon and Schuster, 1982).

Martin Esslin, *The Theatre of The Absurd*, 3rd edn (London: Penguin, 1991).

Northrop Frye, *A Natural Perspective: The Development of Shakespearean Comedy and Romance* (New York: Columbia University Press, 1965).

Walter Kerr, *Tragedy and Comedy* (London: Bodley Head, 1967).

Charles Lamb, 'On The Artificial Comedy of the Last Century', in *Selected Prose*, ed. Adam Phillips (London: Penguin, 1985).

Alexander Leggatt, *English Stage Comedy 1490–1990* (London: Routledge, 1998).

Erich Segal, *The Death of Comedy* (Cambridge, MA: Harvard University Press, 2001).

J. L. Styan, *The Dark Comedy: The Development of Modern Comic Tragedy*, 2nd edn (Cambridge: Cambridge University Press, 1968).

## Film

James Agee, 'Comedy's Greatest Era', *Life* (5 September 1949).

Stanley Cavell, *Pursuits of Happiness: The Hollywood Comedy of Remarriage* (Cambridge, MA: Harvard University Press, 1981).

Noel Carroll, *Comedy Incarnate: Buster Keaton, Physical Humor and Bodily Coping* (Oxford: Wiley-Blackwell, 2007).

Alex Clayton, *The Body in Hollywood Slapstick* (Jefferson, NC: McFarland, 2007).

Alan Dale, *Comedy is a Man in Trouble: Slapstick in the American Movies* (Minneapolis: University of Minnesota Press, 2000).

Raymond Durgnat, *The Crazy Mirror: Hollywood Comedy and the American Image* (London: Faber and Faber, 1969).

Andrew S. Horton, ed., *Comedy, Cinema, Theory* (Berkeley, CA: University of California Press, 1991).

Walter Kerr, *The Silent Clowns* (New York: Knopf, 1975).

## Visual comedy

Jean Clair, ed., *The Great Parade: Portrait of the Artist as Clown* (New Haven: Yale University Press, 2004).

Vic Gatrell, *City of Laughter: Sex and Satire in the Eighteenth-Century London* (London: Atlantic, 2007).

Walter S. Gibson, *Pieter Bruegel and The Art of Laughter* (Berkeley, CA: University of California Press, 2006).

Richard Godfrey, *James Gillray: The Art of Caricature* (London: Tate, 2001).

Michele Hannoosh, *Baudelaire and Caricature: From the Comic to an Art of Modernity* (University Park: Pennsylvania State University Press, 1992).

C. McPhee and N. Orenstein, *Infinite Jest: Caricature and Satire from Leonardo to Levine* (New York: Yale University Press, 2011).

Angus Trumble, *A Brief History of the Smile* (New York: Perseus, 2004).

## Fools, tricksters, jesters, clowns, stand-ups

Oliver Double, *Stand-Up: On Being a Comedian* (London: Metheun, 1997).

Dario Fo, *The Tricks of The Trade* (New York: Methuen, 1991).

Lewis Hyde, *Trickster Makes the World: How Disruptive Imagination Creates Culture* (London: Canongate, 1998).

Carl Gustav Jung, 'On the Psychology of the Trickster Figure', in *Four Archetypes: Mother, Rebirth, Spirit, Trickster*, tr. R. F. C. Hull (London: Routledge, 2003).

Arthur Koestler, 'The Jester' in *The Act of Creation* (London: Hutchinson, 1964).

Stewart Lee, *How I Escaped My Certain Fate: The Life and Deaths of a Stand-Up Comedian* (London: Faber and Faber, 2010).

Norman Manea, *On Clowns: The Dictator and the Artist* (London: Faber and Faber, 1994).

Louise Peacock, *Serious Play: Modern Clown Performance* (Chicago, IL: Chicago University Press, 2009).

Andrew McConnell Stott, *The Pantomime Life of Joseph Grimaldi* (London: Canongate, 2009).

R. F. Storey, *Pierrots on The Stage of Desire: Nineteenth-Century French Literary Artists and the Comic Pantomime* (Princeton, MA: Princeton University Press, 1992).

Enid Welsford, *The Fool: His Social and Literary History* (New York: Anchor, 1961).

William Willeford, *The Fool and His Scepter: A Study in Clowns and Jester and Their Audience* (Evanston, IL: Northwestern University Press, 1969).

Anton Zijderveld, *Reality in a Looking-Glass: Rationality through an Analysis of Traditional Folly* (London: Routledge and Kegan Paul, 1982).

## Religious perspectives

Giorgio Agamben, 'Comedy', in *The End of the Poem*, tr. Daniel Heller-Roazen (Stanford, CA: Stanford University Press, 1999).

Peter Berger, *Redeeming Laughter: The Comic Dimension of Human Experience* (Berlin and New York: Walter de Gruter, 1997).

Harvey Cox, *The Feast of Fools: A Theological Essay on Festivity and Fantasy* (New York: Harper and Row, 1969).

Northrop Frye, 'The Argument of Comedy', in *English Institute Essays: 1948*, ed. D. A. Robertson (New York: Columbia University Press, 1949).

Ingvild Gilhus, *Laughing Gods, Weeping Virgins: Laughter in the History of Religion* (London: Routledge, 1997).

M. A. Screech, *Laughter at the Foot of the Cross* (London: Allen Lane, 1997).

## Psychology/Psychoanalysis

Christopher Bollas, 'Cracking Up' in *Cracking Up: The Work of Unconscious Experience* (New York: Hill and Wang, 1995).

Sandor Ferenczi, 'Laughter' (1913), in *Final Contributions to the Problems and Methods of Psychoanalysis*, tr. Eric Mosbacher (London: Karnac, 2002).

Sigmund Freud, *The Joke and Its Relation to The Unconscious*, tr. Joyce Crick (London: Penguin, 2002).

Sigmund Freud, 'Humour', in *The Penguin Freud Reader*, ed. Adam Phillips (London: Penguin, 2006).

Norman N. Holland, *Laughing: A Psychology of Humour* (Ithaca & London: Cornell University Press, 1982).

Adam Phillips, 'Jokes Apart', in *Promises, Promises* (London: Faber and Faber, 2000).

Adam Phillips, 'On Being Laughed At', in *Equals* (London: Faber and Faber, 2002).

## Theories and philosophical thoughts

Theodor Adorno, 'Is Art Lighthearted?' in *Notes to Literature: Volume II*, tr. Shierry Weber Nicholsen (New York: Columbia University Press, 1992).

W. H. Auden, 'Notes on the Comic' in *The Dyer's Hand* (New York: Vintage, 1968).

Mikhail Bakhtin, *Rabelais and His World* (1965), tr. Helene Iswolsky (Bloomington, IN: Indiana University Press, 1984).

F. H. Buckley, *The Morality of Laughter* (Ann Arbor: University of Michigan Press, 2003).

G. K. Chesterton, entry on 'Humour' for the *Encyclopedia Britannica* (1938).

Samuel Taylor Coleridge, 'Wit and Humor', in *Miscellaneous Criticism*, ed. Thomas Middleton Raysor (London: Constable, 1936).

Terry Eagleton, 'Carnival and Comedy: Bakhtin and Brecht', in *Walter Benjamin, or Towards a Revolutionary Criticism* (London: Verso, 1981).

Max Eastman, *Enjoyment of Laughter* (1936; repr. New Brunswick, NJ: Transaction, 2009).

Ralph Waldo Emerson, 'The Comic' in *Letters and Social Aims* (London: Chatto & Windus, 1876).

Northrop Frye, 'The Mythos of Spring: Comedy', *Anatomy of Criticism: Four Essays* (Princeton, NJ: Princeton University Press, 1957).

R. B. Gill, 'Why Comedy Laughs: The Shape of Laughter and Comedy', *Literary Imagination*, 8. 2 (Spring 2006), pp. 233–50.

Eric Griffiths, 'Ludwig Wittgenstein and the comedy of errors', in *English Comedy*, eds. Michael Cordner, Peter Holland and John Kerrigan (Cambridge: Cambridge University Press, 1994).

William Hazlitt, 'On Wit and Humour' (1819), in *Lectures on the English Comic Writers*, in *The Complete Works of William Hazlitt*, ed. P. P. Howe, 21 vols. (London: Dent, 1930–34).

Thomas Hobbes, ch. 8, sec. 13 of 'Human Nature', in *English Works*: Volume 4, ed. William Molesworth (London: Bohn, 1840).

Frances Hutcheson, *Reflections Upon Laughter* (Glasgow: Baxter, 1750).

Immanuel Kant, Book II, sec. 54 of *Critique of the Power of Judgement* (1790), tr. Paul Guyer and Eric Matthews (Cambridge: Cambridge University Press, 2001).

Søren Kierkegaard, *Concluding Unscientific Postscript* to Philosophical Fragments, Volume 1, ed. and tr. Howard V. Hong and Edna H. Hong (Princeton: Princeton University Press, 1992).

Susanne Langer, 'The Comic Rhythm', in *Feeling and Form* (London: Routledge and Kegan Paul, 1953).

Wyndham Lewis, *The Complete Wild Body* (Santa Barbara: Black Sparrow Press, 1982).

George Meredith, *An Essay on Comedy and The Uses of The Comic Spirit* (1877), in *Comedy*, ed. Wylie Sypher (Baltimore: Johns Hopkins University Press, 1980).

Thomas Nagel, 'The Absurd', in *Mortal Questions* (Cambridge: Cambridge University Press, 1979).

Friedrich Nietzsche, *The Gay Science*, tr. Walter Kaufmann (New York: Vintage, 1974).

Thomas C. Oden, ed., *The Humor of Kierkegaard: An Anthology* (Princeton, NJ: Princeton University Press, 2004).

Luigi Pirandello, *On Humor* (1920), tr. Antonio Illiano and Daniel P. Testa (Chapel Hill, NC: University of North Carolina Press, 1977).

Jean Paul Richter, *Horn of Oberon: Jean Paul Richter's School for Aesthetics*, ed. Margaret R. Hale (Detroit: Wayne State University Press, 1973).

Lord Shaftesbury, *Characteristics of Men, Manners, Opinions, Times* (1711), ed. L. Klein (Cambridge: Cambridge University Press, 1999).

Marie Collins Swabey, *Comic Laughter: A Philosophical Essay* (New Haven: Yale University Press, 1961).

Alenka Zupančič, *The Odd One In: On Comedy* (Cambridge, MA: MIT Press, 2008).

# Index

Index

Index

# ENGLISH LITERATURE
## A Very Short Introduction
Jonathan Bate

Sweeping across two millennia and every literary genre, acclaimed scholar and biographer Jonathan Bate provides a dazzling introduction to English Literature. The focus is wide, shifting from the birth of the novel and the brilliance of English comedy to the deep Englishness of landscape poetry and the ethnic diversity of Britain's Nobel literature laureates. It goes on to provide a more in-depth analysis, with close readings from an extraordinary scene in King Lear to a war poem by Carol Ann Duffy, and a series of striking examples of how literary texts change as they are transmitted from writer to reader.

www.oup.com/vsi

# TRAGEDY
## A Very Short Introduction
### Adrian Poole

What do we mean by 'tragedy' in present-day usage? When we turn on the news, does a report of the latest atrocity have any connection with the masterpieces of Sophocles, Shakespeare and Racine? What has tragedy been made to mean by dramatists, story-tellers, critics, philosophers, politicians and journalists over the last two and a half millennia? Why do we still read, re-write, and stage these old plays?

This book argues for the continuities between 'then' and 'now'. Addressing questions about belief, blame, mourning, revenge, pain, witnessing, timing and ending, Adrian Poole demonstrates the age-old significance of our attempts to make sense of terrible suffering.

www.oup.com/vsi